WORLDS APART:

British Columbia Schools,
Politics, and Labour Relations
Before and After 1972

Thomas Fleming

Thomas Fleming

Thomas Fleming is an emeritus professor in educational history and policy at the University of Victoria. Dr. Fleming has written numerous books and articles on school and administrative history. He co-authored *A History of Thought and Practice in Educational Administration*, a study that has become a standard reference work in the history of school management in the United States. He is also well known for his edited volume, *School Leadership: Essays on the British Columbia School Experience, 1872-1995*, as well as for six other books on school effectiveness, class size, and educational reform. The main focus of his research since the mid-1980s has been the history of children, teachers, school organizations, and administrators in British Columbia about which he has published more than three dozen articles and three books. *The Principal's Office and Beyond: School Leadership in British Columbia, 1849-2005, Volume 1 and Volume 2*, was published in December 2010. Dr. Fleming's documentary history of provincial schooling, *School Days: Voices From British Columbia's Educational Past, 1849-2005*, was published in March 2011.

Dr. Fleming was appointed editor-in-chief and one of six research directors for the 1987-1988 British Columbia Royal Commission on Education and was responsible for writing the commission's main report, *A Legacy for Learners*, editing the *Commissioned Papers of the Royal Commission, Volumes 1-7*, and researching and co-writing *Volume 1: British Columbia Schools and Society*.

No stranger to the real world of administration, Dr. Fleming managed several private-sector companies before serving as Assistant to the President at both the University of Victoria and the University of British Columbia. From 2000 to 2006, he directed the Canadian International Development Agency's Basic Education Program in Rosario, Argentina, that adapted Canadian expertise in modernizing educational conditions for 350 teachers and more than 5,000 youngsters in six of the country's poorest schools. In recognition for this work, he received the University of Victoria Craigdarroch Award in 2006 for Research Contributing to Social Service. He was also awarded the University of Victoria Faculty of Education Inaugural Excellence in Teaching Award in 2000.

WORLDS APART:

British Columbia Schools,
Politics, and Labour Relations
Before and After 1972

Thomas Fleming

BENDALL BOOKS
Educational Publishers

WORLDS APART:

British Columbia Schools, Politics, and Labour Relations Before and After 1972

Thomas Fleming

Set in Adobe Minion Pro

Printed in Canada by Friesens Corporation

First printing: 2011

Third printing: 2012

Library and Archives Canada Cataloguing in Publication

Fleming, Thomas, 1944-

Worlds apart : British Columbia schools, politics and labour relations before and after 1972 / Thomas Fleming.

Includes bibliographical references and index.

ISBN 978-0-9865828-1-3

1. Public schools--Government policy--British Columbia--History.

2. Teachers--Government policy--British Columbia--History.

3. Teachers' unions--British Columbia--History.

4. Education and state--British Columbia--History. I. Title.

LC91.2.B7F64 2011   379.71   C2011-905100-1

BENDALL BOOKS *Educational Publishers*

CANADA: P.O. Box 115, Mill Bay, BC V0R 2P0

E-MAIL: Bendallbooks@islandnet.com

WEB: www.islandnet.com/bendallbooks

FAX: 250-743-2910

*To Fiona McLaughlin and John Fleming
for all the reasons*

Contents

Acknowledgements

My appreciation of the real world of the public schools has been greatly improved over the years by dozens of educators I've interviewed during a twenty-five year period from the early 1980s to the mid-2000s. Former teachers, principals, school inspectors, superintendents, and other educational officers at provincial and local levels talked in lengthy interviews about the schools they attended as youngsters, the teachers and professors who taught them, the pilgrimages they made to the far ends of the province in search of educational work, the communities they lived in, the people they met, and the various stages that comprised their careers. Their recollections have greatly enriched the province's educational history by adding colour and context to an already rich storehouse of primary and secondary sources that constitute British Columbia's educational record. I am particularly indebted to these individuals for the portraits of the pre-1972 educational community they provided and for their descriptions about the great vitality of the public school system in earlier times.

My understanding of the educational past likewise owes much to my colleagues in school history, as well as in other areas of historical study. University of British Columbia (UBC) historian, Robert McDonald, read an early draft of this discussion and raised many thoughtful questions about comparative developments in other areas of government and administration. Patrick Dunae, Emeritus Professor at Vancouver Island University (formerly Malaspina University-College) was extremely helpful in pointing out connections between the British Columbia Teachers' Federation (BCTF) and organized labour, as well as instances of educators in politics in the mid-twentieth century.

Alastair Glegg and Helen Raptis, comrades-in-arms at the University of Victoria (UVic), offered valuable suggestions about sharpening the language and ideas found in the discussion. Long-time school superintendent, Terry McBurney, a veteran of both pre-1972 and post-1972 school eras, reviewed the manuscript and shared his views about the dramatic changes that have characterized the educational world during these two periods. I would also like to express my appreciation to Barry Anderson and Jerry Mussio, two former senior civil servants, for their observances about life in educational government in the post-1972 era and for their general insights into the problems that modern school governance and administration present.

Finally, I would like to express my thanks to UBC emeritus professors, J.D. Wilson and William Bruneau, who encouraged me to expand what was originally a long essay destined for a historical journal into a small monograph. This format will hopefully reach a larger public audience and, in so doing, prompt a much-needed public debate about the organizational and political conflicts that have disrupted British Columbia's schools for some time and that continue to imperil public education. Readers will also note my obvious reliance on William Bruneau's seminal study of the BCTF's history completed in the late 1970s. Another comprehensive and careful historical study of the federation's development, including its labour, social, and political aspirations since the 1960s, is certainly worthy of scholarly attention and long overdue.

Thomas Fleming

Introduction

Little has been written about the conflict between provincial governments and the British Columbia Teachers' Federation (BCTF), a conflict that has been, without question, the single most defining characteristic of public education in the province for the past four decades. It is time that the roots of this conflict were examined. It is also time for British Columbians—in and outside public education—to ask themselves if they would like a future better than this troubled past.

The following historical narrative explores the origins of this longstanding conflict by examining the nature of the organizational relationships in British Columbia's public school sector—and the social contexts that shaped them—during two distinct historical eras, from 1872 to 1972, and the 40-year period since 1972. During the first 100 years, the governance, administrative and other organizational structures that supported public schooling, an institution still modest in size and structure, were remarkably effective. They made the province's schools among the best in the nation and public schooling an institution of immense provincial pride. For various reasons, the post-1972 educational world evolved into a world of "school wars" where a once-harmonious educational community was riven by politics, special interests, conflicts, and organizational distrust. Some factors that produced this recent and unhappy era were structural in origin. Old governance and administrative arrangements that proved serviceable during the nineteenth century and the first half of the twentieth century have increasingly seemed incapable of addressing the organizational and other complexities that characterize modern schools and educational systems.

Other factors have also been at work. The post-1972 expansion of the school's mandate into the social domain, the rise of special interest politics, the decline in school populations, and shifting provincial demographics have all strained institutional relationships and exposed fundamental insufficiencies in the structures that once governed and supported public schools. Although the quality of public education has remained basically sound, a steady stream of complaints about alleged inadequacies in educational finance and school resources, a breakdown in educational labour relations, and four decades of partisan and political infighting about educational policies have produced not only a profoundly distressed public system but also a lack of confidence among British Columbians about the quality and future of public schooling.

This historical essay is intended to provoke questions about the organizational structures that currently exist and the strained relationships that bedevil the province's most important educational organizations—the government and its education ministry, the BCTF, and the British Columbia School Trustees Association (BCSTA). This essay is not intended, directly or inferentially, to question the quality of the public system, or the efforts of tens of thousands of dedicated individuals who work as teachers, administrators, and in other capacities.

It is intended, however, to provide a non-varnished view of the events and politics that have conspired to bring the once-great institution of public education to its knees over the past 40 years. Admittedly, the discussion that follows is generally critical in its assessments of the province's major educational organizations, the way they behave, and the motivations underlying their actions. Looking back over the developments of recent decades, there is, to be sure, more than enough blame to share. If it wished, government could no doubt take delight in the shortsightedness of school boards, their clumsiness in managing budgets, and the vanity of some of their members—not to mention the puffery, self-righteousness, and blind ambition so often characteristic of BCTF executives. So, too, could school board members and teacher representatives revel in the obvious confusion and lack of purpose in an education ministry that has floundered since the 1970s, in governments on both sides of the aisle too timid to show any form of real leadership in public education. Or, equally, in the marginalization of the co-governed agency created by statute to bargain on behalf of school boards, the British Columbia Public School Employers' Association (BCPSEA), an organization confined to the sidelines on occasion while politicians conducted last-minute bargaining deals to secure educational peace at any price, no matter how costly or short-lived.

But rather than celebrate the sins of others, government officials, teacher executives, and members of the province's major educational organizations may wish to consider some of the questions prompted by this historical review. For example:

Are the organizational relationships in British Columbia's public school sector really in the depressing state of repair as described here or are they better or worse than this?

Is a long-term truce between government and the teachers' federation feasible, or should the current governance, administrative, and financial structures in schooling be dismantled so we can start again?

Can government and the teacher's federation find a way to establish a meaningful accord given the historical baggage they both carry and the climate of distrust that now exists?

Can school politics and labour relations be conducted in a more civilized manner and without the demonization that all too frequently marks educational disputes?

And, last but not least, can British Columbia educators and the organizations that represent them learn from their own troubled history or are they destined to perpetuate the conflict that so badly divides the schools?

One small postscript is required. Discerning readers may wonder why faculties of education have escaped what some may consider an abrasive assessment of other educational organizations in the province. This is not a matter of favoritism but of perspective and judgment. Faculties of education have simply not been feature players in the turbulent public school story of recent decades. With few exceptions, most faculties of education and most education professors have had little impact on the public schools, or public policy, since the mid-1970s. Up to this time, important educational gatherings of public school folk were routinely opened with the benediction of an education dean or an important academic figure in education.

Since then, however, everything has changed. Few people in today's teaching or administrative fraternity, much less those who comprise the ranks of school trustees, federation executives, or district and government officials, could name even one education dean at the four largest provincial universities. Historian Barbara Tuchman's colourful assessment of the social sciences as "an isolation ward of unintelligibility" may equally describe modern education faculties to those in the "real world of the public schools," as practitioners like to describe themselves. Distracted by phenomenological debates of medieval proportions, along with crusades for myriad social causes, education faculties have lost much of the credibility they once enjoyed in solving the instructional and organizational problems of schools. The decline of their influence is a sad story in itself—and one worth recounting another day.

Historical Research

A few brief notes on historical inquiry are in order before this narrative begins. In commenting on questions of current interest, historical research enjoys certain advantages and limitations. History's great advantage lies in its capacity to bring meaning and understanding to past events, to provide detailed description of people and circumstances at particular places and times, and to furnish perspective about relationships among people, organizations, and events in ways unavailable to participants at the time.

By establishing context, analyzing and evaluating original documents, and assembling social facts about human experiences, historical research provides a tapestry of understanding about individual lives and, in this case, organizational worlds now vanished from memory. Of all the disciplines, history is perhaps the most adept at providing ways of seeing the complexities of earlier generations and societies "in the round." Historical study is also remarkably useful in illustrating how social perceptions of issues and events change according to time, place, and context. Seeing the world historically offers a way of appreciating the past on its own terms, as it was experienced by those who lived through it, rather than in terms imposed by the present. In such ways, history is instructive in the differences and comparisons it forces us to consider.

French historian Marc Bloch celebrated historical research for the "subtle enchantment of the unfamiliar" it presented.[1] British novelist L.P. Hartley has similarly reminded us "the past is a foreign country, they do things differently there." Conversely, when we fail to appreciate where we have come from, or to understand the journey we are on, we remain unaware of the invisible baggage we carry from the past and the invisible chains that restrict our ideas, our behaviours, and our structures. Historical study, and the perspective it affords across time, place, and culture, furnishes a platform for us to examine what is relevant and of value from more than one angle of vision.

History also has its limitations. Historical investigations do not always address social and other questions in terms deemed relevant by the present. Things past and present are not always equal and, therefore, cannot be meaningfully compared. Historical research may also be "silent" on some questions of current controversy, and remain so until historians find sufficient cause to initiate the slow task of reconstructing the context and events of another time to explain how issues or questions of contemporary interest evolved, or were understood in earlier eras.

For instance, in this research, efforts have been made to note the incomparability in the purposes and functions of nineteenth-century and twentieth-century high schools, along with differences in the governance and administrative structures that supported them. Likewise, the discussion has tried to underscore important differences that must be kept in mind when comparing the original, and rather plain, organizational features of British Columbia's earliest public school system with the elaborate bureaucratic structures characteristic of far larger and more complex twentieth and twenty-first century systems.

One final but important point should be made in this brief synopsis. School history in British Columbia is a remarkably well-developed subject compared to the historical study of education in many other provincial, state, and national jurisdictions. Since the mid-1960s, the province's educational history has been well chronicled by some two-dozen academic scholars in the province's universities, supported by strong contingents of graduate and undergraduate students working in the provincial archives.

Together, these researchers have produced a robust tradition of inquiry into children, teachers, schools, educational leaders, and school organizations that is envied by educational historians in Europe, the United States, and elsewhere. For many years, British Columbia has also been fortunate in having a small brigade of private, local, and amateur historians who have examined various issues in public and private educational sectors, and who have charted the origins and development of many individual schools. Taken as a whole, this community of academic and private historians has produced a rich secondary literature that has illuminated many facets of the province's educational past since the time that the first colonial school opened in 1849. Several comprehensive bibliographies and historiographies reveal the broad scope and impressive depth of these investigations.[2]

Underpinning much of this research is a large compendium of primary historical documents preserved as part of the education ministry's records (formerly the education department and, still earlier, the education office) and now archived by the Royal British Columbia Museum Corporation. Briefly summarized, these include nearly 140 years of annual departmental reports on the schools, inspectors' reports on teachers and schools, teachers' bureau reports, reports and briefs submitted to royal and other educational commissions, official correspondence, news clipping files, photographic files, along with countless pages of description about curricular and instructional developments. Many of these documents can be readily found using Patrick Dunae's volume, *The School Record: A Guide to Government Archives Relating to Public Education in British Columbia, 1852-1946.*[3]

In its conclusions and interpretations, the following narrative is consistent with the main body of educational history research in British Columbia. As the endnotes attest, I remain indebted to many colleagues who have reconstructed parts of the province's educational and social history, as well as to Canadian historians generally, for the broader understandings of the national past that guide this work.

The discussion that follows is presented in three chapters. Chapters 1 and 2 describe the pre-1972 and post-1972 worlds of the public schools and the social and educational circumstances that defined them. They chronicle the public school's earliest foundations, the forces that animated public education during the first century of its development in British Columbia, its bureaucratization and maturity as an agency of state in the twentieth century, the steady expansion of the school's educational and social mandate after World War II, and the post-1970s collapse of both the educational community and the broad public consensus that long supported public schools. Chapter 3 explores recent factors that have reshaped the public school's mission as well as the organizational disconnections and other developments that now diminish the public school's place in provincial life and challenge the future of public schooling.

Notes

1. Marc Bloch, *The Historian's Craft* (Manchester: Manchester University Press, 1954), 7-9, 17-18.

2. See, for example, bibliographies of educational history regularly published by *BC Studies and Historical Studies in Education,* or earlier works such as Valerie Giles, *Annotated Bibliography of Education History in British Columbia: A Royal British Columbia Museum Technical Report* (Victoria: Royal British Columbia Museum, 1992). Vancouver Island University also offers a substantial and easy to access collection of sources related to research in British Columbia's school history through its electronic site, "The Homeroom." See: http://www.viu.ca/homeroom/content/resource/

3. Patrick A. Dunae, *The School Record: A Guide to Government Archives Relating to Public Education in British Columbia 1852-1946* (Victoria: Ministry of Government Services, 1992).

One of the earliest educational photographs in British Columbia shows a man, woman, and a dog in front of the Springside Road School in Sooke on lower Vancouver Island in the 1870s. During much of the century that would follow, rural schools reflected domestic architecture in their style and manner of construction. **Courtesy British Columbia Archives E-03887.**

CHAPTER 1

The Common School's Ascendancy

The institution we know today as public schooling was born in the second half of the nineteenth century in a floodtide of civic optimism about the exhilarating possibilities of state-supported education. Across North America, as well as Great Britain, a diverse coalition of politicians, community leaders, newspaper editors, intellectuals, and citizens at large found common cause to endorse publicly funded schools. Their reasons were many. Public schools, Victorian social reformers proclaimed, could act as an institutional panacea. More than just instructing children in the rudiments of reading, writing, and arithmetic, they could also help banish, or at least reduce, civic ignorance, encourage a higher level of public morality, and generally assist in a broad social movement to uplift society. Schooling was equated with progress and with the Christian mission of redeeming society or "salvaging the lower classes," as historian Susan Houston bluntly put it.[1] According to the liberal social crusaders of the time, the schools seemed destined to emerge as "museums of virtue," to use sociologist Willard Waller's eloquent phrase, radiant in their possibilities of improving social life.[2]

Both the Empire, and Canada's development as a nation state, could equally be served by the introduction of common schools. Egerton Ryerson, the chief architect of Ontario's provincial system, declared that the task of the public school was "to impart to the public mind . . . useful knowledge based upon . . . sound Christian principles . . . [and] to render the Educational system . . . the indirect but powerful instrument of British Constitutional Government."[3] Ryerson, like other nineteenth-century educational statesmen, including Thomas Jefferson in the U.S. and Thomas Babbington Macaulay in England, shared a broadly-held belief that an educated citizenry served as the "best security of a good government and constitutional liberty."[4] Without the right schooling, Ryerson reckoned, people risked becoming "the slaves of despots and the dupes of demagogues."[5]

In the social imagination that ignited Victorian liberalism on both sides of the Atlantic, aspirations for the common school seemed boundless.[6] Schools could prepare children for the world of work, assimilate the poor and foreign-born, civilize society in general, inculcate in pupils a sense of provincial and national identity, and prevent crime, delinquency, and idleness by keeping youngsters off the streets. "The middle classes know," Lord Shaftesbury of England's upper chamber remarked, "that the safety of their lives and property depends upon their having round them a peaceful, happy, and moral population."[7] In the face of untrammeled industrial and urban growth—where family, church, and community seemed to falter in providing social stability—public schooling promised to provide a state of social equilibrium by equalizing children's social and intellectual development, and by providing a level of socialization that would minimize family and individual differences.[8] Simply put, from its earliest beginnings the educational and social agenda set for public schooling was comprehensive and highly ambitious. More than any other civic institution of the day, the common school seemed best suited to achieve the progress, order, and prosperity that fired the liberal soul. As historian G.M. Young rightfully observed about British schools: "*The Education Act* of 1870 was, for most English people, the first sensible impact of the administrative state on their private lives."[9]

In British Columbia, the crusade to secure free public education first had to overcome strongly entrenched denominational and class-based educational and social structures. Schooling began on Canada's west coast in 1849 when the Hudson's Bay Company (HBC) made provision for a school at Fort Victoria, a bulwark constructed seven years earlier to solidify its economic presence in the Pacific Northwest following American incursions into the Oregon territory. In short order, several HBC schools were built to provide for the education of officers' and labourers' children, albeit separately. Rounding out the educational establishment in the new colony were two Roman Catholic schools, as well as a handful of other institutions operating under the auspices of the Church of England. Both the Anglican and HBC schools, according to UBC historian Jean Barman, clearly reflected a transfer of English educational structures and practices to the new world, replete with "clear class and religious divisions."[10] As Barman observed: "In the new colony as in England, education was perceived as having two prime functions: preparation to maintain existing place within the social order, and inculcation of denominational religious beliefs."[11]

The quiet that marked this outpost of empire on the southern tip of Vancouver Island was shattered in 1857 with the discovery of gold on the Fraser River's gravel bars.[12] Within a few short years, some 25,000 newcomers disembarked in Victoria en route to the mainland's gold fields amid a frenzied rush for riches and adventure.[13] The newcomers came from far and wide. Some were from Ontario and the Maritimes, who ventured west in search of their fortunes. Some hailed from South Africa, Australia, California, and other states in the Union. In the main, they were far more democratic in spirit than the colonial authorities or the colonies' first settlers. Before long, the crown colony of Vancouver Island—and a mainland colony that assumed crown colony status in 1858—were embroiled in disputes between political and civic interests that favoured "fee paying" and denominational schooling and those who demanded a system of "free and non-sectarian" education. As Barman has illustrated, the struggle continued with great vigour until the mid-1860s when gradually a consensus began to emerge that a publicly supported, non-denominational school system was best suited for the soon-to-be-province.[14]

The public's conversion to the idea of a free and public system was variously conditioned. Earlier developments in eastern Canada and the United States greatly shaped a climate favourable to universal schooling a continent away on Canada's west coast. Frustration with the "irregular pattern" of educational offerings in the two colonies, the collapse of free-school legislative efforts in 1865 and 1869, and the generally deplorable state of colonial schools, had also helped energize a movement for a free school system.[15] Spirited newspaper campaigns on behalf of non-sectarian schools conducted by newspaper editors Amor de Cosmos in Victoria and John Robson in New Westminster substantially eroded the traditional influence of church and colonial authorities, thereby advancing the cause for educational change. No one was more confident than de Cosmos about the educational future that lay within the public's grasp: state schools for everyone, he proclaimed, would break down "old country ideas" about "the servility of one class to another," a notion he regarded as "sickening enough at all times" but especially "repugnant [in the] soil of a new land."[16]

When *An Act Respecting Public Schools* was passed on April 22, 1872, it embodied two principal ideas—that public schools should enjoy government support and that private and denominational schools should not.[17] Neither this school act nor subsequent legislation, however, ever questioned the "legitimacy, or for that matter, the desirability of non-public schools."[18] And, so, for a century to come, public schooling grew and developed, as UBC's Lorne Downey pointed out, "largely unchallenged by supporters of other forms of education."[19] Despite the near-monopolistic status the public school came to enjoy, it failed, nevertheless, to extinguish a persistent demand in certain social quarters for schools that were private, religious, or alternative. British Columbia's non-public school sector, or what Downey called public education's "ideological alternative," continued to soldier along in a small but parallel educational universe from the 1870s to the 1970s, composed mainly of two kinds of schools—Roman Catholic and elite private schools.[20] Not until passage of Bill 33 in 1977, *The Independent Schools Support Act*, did the provincial government fully serve notice that it intended to support educational choice outside the public sector.[21]

In their imperial and centralist character, early school acts in British Columbia reflected the essence of school legislation in Ontario and the Maritimes.[22] These bodies of legislation have been described this way:

> These legislative enactments . . . invariably held that only a strong central authority could provide the vision and control necessary to establish provincial education across unorganized and, in some cases, vast territories with diverse populations and uncertain economic prospects. They empowered, in law, government ministers, or councils of public instruction comprised of cabinet officers, to serve as the ultimate policy and decision-making authority in schooling, and allowed these individuals or groups to intervene in any matter, at any level, for the good of the system. Such legislation commonly made clear that provincial government officials and their staffs would be liberated from the problem of actually delivering school services; this responsibility would accrue to local boards of trustees and their staffs who were, in the final analysis, 'creatures of provincial authority,' and ever 'subject to the constant scrutiny and, if warranted, intervention' of provincial officers.[23]

Moreover, because schooling was equated with progress, it "could not be left to chance," as Houston pointed out.[24] Historian Marvin Lazerson explained it more directly: "Without regular attendance, there would be illiteracy and no moral code, and thus continued social disorganization and criminality. Attendance was necessary, moreover, to justify the increasingly elaborate organizational and training mechanisms that had become central to public education."[25] Early educational authorities in British Columbia, UBC historian F. Henry Johnson observed, "were engaged in a constant struggle to impress upon parents and school boards the necessity of having all school-age children attend school and attend it regularly."[26] Accordingly, rules to make pupil attendance compulsory were introduced by provincial governments through various laws and amendments from the 1870s to the mid-twentieth century.[27] In British Columbia, it was not until 1923 that more than 80 per cent of the enrolled population attended classes daily.[28] No single action likely prescribed the quintessential character of public schooling as much as making attendance compulsory. It guaranteed, at once, the hegemony of the state in private and family life, the viability of the public system as a securely funded educational enterprise with little competition and, no doubt unintentionally, the virtual life-long tenure of public sector employment for teachers and administrators.[29]

Along with amendments to ensure compulsory attendance, regulations were also introduced to control admission into the teaching profession. Provincial education departments established normal schools for teacher preparation and established certificates to denote differences in teachers' qualifications. At face value, "state" or "public" underwriting of schooling seemed to offer considerable technical advantages over the highly idiosyncratic and, occasionally, chaotic state of private education. Everyone would pay and everyone would benefit. Public support would be transparent and predictable. Moreover, public schools could standardize their operations by following a common curriculum, taught by a commonly trained cohort of teachers who would employ a set of common instructional methods. So, too, could the public schools operate with commonly applied legislative provisions that would regulate teacher and other behaviours across local jurisdictions to achieve common educational outcomes, shared by all children commonly, in what was deemed to be the common or public good. Nothing, in fact, appeared to be more egalitarian or socially just than the notion of commonality that rested at the heart of the public school.

Such developments dramatically remanufactured the landscape of educational provision. A half-century before industrial engineers routinely standardized assembly practices in North American factories, fledgling school systems across the continent were already standardizing the contents and methods of instruction, indicators of pupil progress and participation, and introducing ever-more exacting measures of cost and efficiency. Along with the factory and the business corporation, the public school easily earned the right to be considered as one of the three great organizational inventions of the nineteenth century. In the age that lay ahead, civic faith in the public school would remain undaunted and untested in any fundamental way. Criticism, for the most part, would be unknown. Public schooling would blossom, bolstered by a broad public consensus about schooling that would, according to Barman, "endure virtually unaltered for almost a century."[30]

A Century of Triumph

A simple but effective governance and administrative system underpinned the public school's success. Confederation in 1871 had conferred complete statutory control over schools into the hands of provincial authorities. Accordingly, the province was empowered to: assign school texts and set the curriculum; examine, appoint, and inspect teachers; define, appeal, alter, or amend school district boundaries; allocate funds for school support; and intervene in any matter at any time for the good of the system. All the functional levers required for directing the course of public education were in the hands of the province. The "Free School Act" of 1872, as the first school legislation was popularly known, made it clear that the government's Education Office would govern and administer the system from on high. Local boards of education, comprised of elected trustees, would actually deliver school programs and services in communities around the province and, in so doing, represent community interests and priorities.

This separation of responsibilities was immensely practical. Given the province's vast size (950,000 square kilometers), its daunting and mountainous topography, the great distances between settlements, and no more than a handful of roads that pushed hesitantly into the province's interior, it was impossible for educational government to do anything but manage the new school system by remote control. Providing—and administering—common schooling for the more than 1,700 youngsters of disparate origins scattered across the province that the new school system inherited from the colonial regime would prove no easy matter.

As John Jessop, the province's first superintendent of schools, calculated at the end of his first year in the job, some 250 boys and 162 girls were attending 21 multi-graded schools across the public system, 900 children were not attending any school, and 200 or so were located in the "Upper Country" where no schools were "within their reach."[31] About the clap-board schoolhouses he found scattered across tiny communities, Jessop concluded: "Children somewhat disorderly and ... little attention paid to teacher. Discipline and arrangement of studies very deficient. Reading and spelling not creditable. For want of books, a large class, not far enough advanced for Third Reader, were reading in the Fifth."[32] "The question as to how the educational wants of the interior of this Province are to be supplied," he noted anxiously in his report of 1872, "is one that I approach under a deep sense of the responsibility involved in attempting to deal with it."[33] Clearly, this rag-tag assembly of schools required deft organization if it was ever to become a single common "system."

Because government's statutory powers far exceeded the province's actual "hands-on" capacity to influence local educational events, Jessop and the superintendents who followed him designed an uncomplicated management information system that would let them see into the state of schools—and administer them—from afar.[34] Using the teacher's register as the system's basic instrument of record, a pyramid of statistical information was assembled that, when aggregated, provided class, school, district, and provincial level summaries of pupils' attendance and progress, the number of reports sent to parents and school officials, the number of youngsters disciplined, suspended, expelled, or truant, and other sundry matters—on a daily, weekly, monthly, or yearly basis, as required. After 1887, when the school inspectorate was first established, the accuracy of the reports upon which government's paper empire was constructed could be confirmed or denied by first-hand visits to schools by a corps of inspectors.[35] In effect, the entire institution of provincial schooling could be managed—and was—by remote control from the Education Office (later the provincial education department) on Victoria's Government Street.[36]

Strict statutory control and timely information allowed Jessop and his successors to oversee and effectively manage what remained for many years a simple but proficient organizational model—and a model remarkably modest in its aspirations. For the first three-quarters of a century in the province's history—certainly until the early 1950s—Jessop's dream that the province's common schools, which he envisioned as colleges for the people, would assume a common and humble shape familiar to many later generations of British Columbians. From the coast to the Rockies, sparse and often dilapidated one-room schoolhouses, attended by 10 to 12 youngsters, would emerge as the chief centres for learning in a vast and defiant land that Barman has insightfully termed "The West Beyond the West."[37]

From the 1870s to the 1930s, these small and unprepossessing schools swelled in number from a couple of dozen to more than 800.[38] In fact, until 1927, two-thirds of provincial school districts consisted of no more than one ungraded elementary school, staffed by a single teacher, and attended by youngsters distributed variously across the grades, regardless of age and ability.

Living on the frontier was still a reality for many British Columbians well into the twentieth century, something graphically illustrated by the fact that nearly half of the province's schools lay outside city or municipal boundaries until the time of the Great Depression. Even as late as 1942, more than half the province's schools were single-room structures featuring a single teacher. Geography, more than any other factor, charted school history's uneven course in British Columbia, at least until the middle of the twentieth century. Until then, two distinct and usually separate constellations of public schools existed in the province—one rural and generally poor and one urban and comparatively far richer.

Rural schools were modest in their aspirations as well as in appearance. Frequently bereft of books, especially in English and social studies, classes in country schools provided a catch-as-catch-can kind of instruction, usually dispensed by inexperienced and inexpensive teachers.[39] As a rule, library facilities were impoverished, instruction in French and other modern languages hard to come by, and home economics and vocational courses usually notable by their absence.[40] Playground and physical education facilities were likewise generally unknown. In many of the province's small communities, pupils were drilled in no more than the basics of reading, writing, and arithmetic, along with whatever else the curriculum would stretch to up to the end of grade 8. In comparison, rural or, at least, non-urban communities with a "superior school" that offered instruction to the end of grade 10 felt blessed during the Depression and war years for the extra two years of learning they could provide.

Progress, too, was straightforwardly determined. Inequity in educational opportunity was viewed as no one's fault, merely a condition of geography to be overcome. In city and country schools alike, improving pupil participation rates year over year, getting more youngsters to attend high school, and generally teaching children to be good citizens were universally considered to be the system's primary goals. Descriptions of pupils as "special" or "exceptional" had yet to enter the educational vocabulary, and notions about "entitlement" were still unknown to teachers, children, or their parents. The great educational challenge prior to 1945 was to fashion a rough-hewn equality across a system that grew in developmental spurts. Few British Columbians complained in the post-1945 era when surging pupil populations meant unsightly "portables," crudely connected annexes, or "swing shifts," where teachers taught morning and afternoon sessions of 120 students divided into four classes.[41]

In its original expression, public schooling's grade structure was far different than what we know today. It consisted simply of a collection of schools that offered instruction from grades 1 to 8. Although the first high school was established in Victoria in 1876—the only institution of its kind west of Winnipeg and north of San Francisco—its principal purpose was to function as a training institution for teachers until a normal school was eventually built. Even though educators and the public today regard elementary and high schools as sequential parts of an overarching kindergarten to grade 12 system, this view was entirely foreign to the nineteenth century. High schools, to Jessop and Victorian society generally, were institutions completely distinct from common schools in both their purposes and in the populations they served. Even the most ardent educational reformers of the 1870s did not envision high schools as institutions to be democratized or, indeed, institutions that should be open to everyone's youngsters. Their mission was something else, namely to offer a level of higher scholarship—and the possibility of an intellectual career in medicine, law, or teaching—to a small percentage of students of demonstrated academic ability.

Although "public" in name and, in large part, publicly-financed, high schools were expected to be selective in character and were widely recognized within Victorian society as unique institutions coupled only loosely with "lower" schools. Because only a small percentage of provincial students ever gained admission to these institutions of advanced learning during the first half-century of their operation, high schools enjoyed a social and educational prominence similar to that enjoyed by today's prestigious universities. Robert Sprott, co-founder of Vancouver's Sprott-Shaw Business Institute in 1904, estimated in 1910 that "scarcely 15 per cent of the youth of the nation go beyond the first year in high school."[42] Even by 1923, 50 years after Jessop established the public schools, fewer than 10 per cent of provincial pupils were attending high school.[43] Looking back to the classrooms of the 1920s and 1930s where he taught, school inspector Wilf Graham recalled the great support that existed for elementary education before the end of World War II.[44] There was far less support beyond that level, he noted, because "many of the boys went out to work."

The notion of connecting the three levels of high school—junior, intermediate, and senior—to the lower "public" or "grade-schools" did not emerge until the 1920s when urban high schools first began to accept "commercial" and "general" students. And, even then, distinguished high schools such as Victoria High and Oak Bay High made it clear that they were still not open to everyone by charging yearly instructional fees of $140 and $175, respectively, large sums of money by standards of the day.[45]

Not until after 1945 were the sightlines of educational progress for many students raised to include the completion of junior matriculation (grade 11). Even by the end of the 1950s, the notion of "high school for everyone," a notion that encouraged the establishment of post-war comprehensive schools, still remained out of reach. As the 1960s began, only about 70 per cent of elementary students continued through school to grade 12.[46] High school completion remained another matter. Even well past mid-century, few educators or parents complained about the classification of high school students across the province into "vocational," "general," and "academic" streams.

A Tradition of Trust

Factors other than the system's organizational structure, simplicity, and modest aspirations also contributed to public schooling's extraordinary success—not the least of which was the generous amount of cooperation and trust that characterized relationships between provincial and local authorities during public education's first century.[47] From the system's earliest beginnings, Education Office staff and trustees scattered in small educational parishes across the province understood and appreciated their mutuality of interests. Government knew it was dependent on trustees and local communities to achieve its educational mission. More particularly, the Education Office relied on trustees to provide educational facilities, govern local schools, hire and pay teachers, and provide the wood, water, and janitorial services that schools required. It also counted on trustees to supply vital wisdom and information about local conditions, to find housing for young and inexperienced teachers, to ensure safe passage for inspectors across surging rivers and treacherous mountain passes, and generally to wait patiently while the province's education officers tried to extend the educational franchise equally to children everywhere.

Alternatively, trustees were no less dependent on government. Trustees knew that the government's men could be counted on to help provision a local school, pay for and round up a teacher in districts where taxes would not cover a teacher's salary, push for a capital allowance to improve schools in good times, and generally keep volunteer trustees on the right side of departmental rules and regulations. Textbooks, globes, and other kinds of instructional paraphernalia, whenever available, were shipped by mail or coach from educational government in Victoria. For the price of a stamp, government, in the form of the superintendent's office, could be counted on to protect local school board interests with land surveyors, public works officials, and even banks.[48]

Correspondence inward and outward from the provincial superintendent's office disclosed the close relationship between trustees and government, along with a spirit of cooperation among all parties.[49] For decades, "hundreds of rural boards remained beholden to the province . . . Indeed the survival of local schools largely depended on the superintendent's good offices."[50] Certainly, until the late 1960s—in some instances even later—relationships between government and many trustee boards were closer than they were between trustee boards and their own provincial association.[51] As UVic historian James London has pointed out, membership in the BCSTA was traditionally tenuous in nature, voluntary in character, and marked by strong patterns of local board independence in "staffing schools," "settling salary agreements," and competing for available teachers in ways that were neither "objective" nor "rational."[52]

Such government benevolence was expected, and could be found, throughout the administrative chain of command. More than once, inspectors turned a blind eye to insufficient class sizes in mud-spattered roadside schools by counting the noses of infants and pets to reach 10—the minimum number required to keep a one-room school open and, more often than not, to keep a local community alive.[53] UBC historian John Calam's reconstruction of Alex Lord's four-year tour of inspection along the north coast and the Peace River Block illustrates the strong inter-personal ties that typified relationships between government's school officers, trustees, and other settlers across what was still a wild frontier.[54] "I knew everyone by name at least 'north of fifty-three,'" Lord later wrote matter-of-factly.[55]

The system, still immature in many respects, was nevertheless fluid and lubricated with goodwill.[56] When nineteenth-century principal Edward B. Paul recounted "the great harmony existing in the Nanaimo schools between trustees, teachers, parents, and pupils," he was engaged in more than customary politeness, or a barefaced attempt to cultivate public relations.[57] Far more likely, he was referring to a genuine spirit of cooperation and a shared sense of purpose—extraordinary no doubt by today's standards—that he observed between educators and the general public at a time before control of educational institutions rested largely in the hands of the professionals who staffed them. Turn-of-the-century Victoria principal Miss Mary Williams in Victoria was no less effusive in recording her "thanks to the Department of Education and trustees for their ready co-operation in any scheme for the well-being of teachers and pupils."[58] Nor was Nanaimo Girls' principal, Miss Maria Lawson, shy about acknowledging the efforts of school board members in her 1895 annual report: "Trustees have in the past year, as in former years, shown themselves to be the kind and considerate friends of the teachers in their employ."[59]

A Community of Educators

Tight connections between educators and communities around schools bespoke a larger network of interlocking local-provincial relationships in which allegiances, many of them life-long, were routinely pledged inside school organizations and between school folk and parents, not to mention many other members of the public outside schools. This web of connections was sustained by the rational organizational structure of the public system and the intricate system of social relations it prescribed from one-room schools to the corridors of government and, beyond them, to the lecture halls of normal schools and universities.

Historically, the path to an educational career ordinarily began by teaching in small single-room schools in remote settlements, sometimes with colourful names such as Anarchist Mountain, Deadman's Creek, Lone Butte, or Pouce Coupé. Then, as educators gained in credentials and experience, they moved from small isolated communities, usually southward, to larger more civilized centres. From their first assignments, teachers became part of an educational circle comprised of other teachers, school inspectors, principals on occasion and, invariably, the local chairpersons and board secretaries who signed the district's cheques. For many years, teaching in much of rural British Columbia remained a migratory occupation.[60] Teachers arrived and moved on with the seasons, few remaining much more than a year or so in remote schools during the end of the nineteenth and the first half of the twentieth century. Securing a position in larger schools and larger communities, or an administrative office, was a routine part of a built-in socialization process that introduced teachers and principals into a wider social and professional universe.

Teacher mobility, however, meant earning an inspector's confidence and maintaining reasonable relations with local trustees and parents. Always on the lookout for individuals of instructional or administrative promise, inspectors were quick to push deserving young teachers forward and to give them advice about further study at one of the two provincial normal schools, or about summer school courses in education offered at the Vancouver Normal School and UBC after 1914 and 1920, respectively. Along with inspectors' recommendations, letters of reference from trustee boards were extremely helpful in finding new and better employment. Such letters were routinely duplicated, forwarded to the registrar in the education department, and filed alongside an inspector's report on a particular teacher's performance. The educational world was distinctly feudal in the way people relied on each other from the bottom to the top of the system.

From the end of World War I to the end of the 1980s, when the government eventually abandoned its role in teacher credentialling, the registrar's office served as an employment clearinghouse for generations of young teachers eager to secure their first appointment. Among the half-dozen individuals who acted as registrar, the most famous, no doubt, was J.L. Watson, who for decades between the wars was the epicentre of the provincial system. The kindly Watson—renowned for his intimate knowledge of the province's rural geography, as well as for his unfailing and prodigious memory—found positions "up-country" for hundreds of youngsters fresh from teachers' college anxious to secure jobs. Longtime provincial educator Bernard Gillie remembered Watson as the "prince of administration," a man who "knew everybody," including the names of teachers' husbands, wives, and other family members.[61] Principal Stewart Graham, the department's "unofficial official" in the Peace River before Bill Plenderleith, the inspector, arrived in 1933, likewise claimed that Watson could recite the name of every teacher in British Columbia in the 1920s and 1930s and knew specific directions to the most remote schools and teacherages in more than 800 districts.[62]

Through the registrar's office and the inspectors, the education department was central to many teachers' lives. It was not, however, the sole institution to shape the public school's organizational culture or the values and behaviours of the educational community. Scholastically important high schools greatly conditioned teachers' academic values and instructional styles, especially at a time when many teachers never enrolled in academic courses beyond normal school. Sometimes, normal schools themselves were enormously influential. Often, teachers corresponded with former normal school instructors asking for assistance years after their training was complete. Decades before he became a BCTF president, Bernard Gillie recalled writing to his normal school master, C.B. Wood, for assistance in teaching "18 new Austrian youngsters" who arrived in his Okanagan classroom "speaking no English".[63]

Last but not least, of course, was the towering influence of UBC in all things intellectual and pedagogical after its opening in 1915. For a half-century, UBC arts and science faculties prepared generations of high school teachers with bachelors and masters degrees, and the annual summer school sessions of its education department—sometimes in league with the province's own education department—provided vital opportunities for working teachers to upgrade their credentials.

Fifty years after the public school system was first established, the educational community remained a small and tightly bound universe. In 1922, fewer than 3,000 teachers paced provincial classrooms, a modest educational corps scarcely more than the population of one large urban high school today.[64] Even by 1947, as the great post-war bull-market in public education was beginning, the number of educators in schools, universities, normal schools, and government barely surpassed 5,000 and the connective tissue linking one-room schoolteachers to senior civil servants in government remained as strong as ever.[65] A set of well-understood bureaucratic structures, "from the lowly classroom teacher to the door of the deputy minister," as UBC historian William Bruneau put it, offered ambitious teachers the possibility of "elevation through the ranks."[66]

Educators drifted from government departments to normal schools and the universities, as well as from government and administrative offices to the BCTF for "leadership training," as Bruneau aptly termed it, before heading back to government again.[67] Ambition was saddled with few constraints. About 80 per cent of the individuals who served as BCTF presidents between 1917 and 1965 were school principals, many from the province's largest and most prestigious urban schools.[68] Bruneau noted the "innumerable journeys on bad roads" made by Kootenay principal and later deputy minister, Frank Levirs, to keep "the BCTF membership roster at full and growing strength during the dark days of the 1930s."[69] Similarly, Dawson Creek principal Stewart Graham recalled his first inspector in the north, Ray McCleod, "horribly wounded in the First World War," who "helped me . . . organize the first local of the BCTF in the Peace River."[70] Before the 1970s, nothing was seen to be amiss when energetic and aspiring teachers stalked backwoods schools in search of a principalship, or when local school leaders jumped from principals' offices to become government inspectors, bureaucrats, or normal school instructors—or who accepted professional leadership positions in the BCTF.

From the time of the Edwardian Age onward, powerful educational figures such as C.G. Brown, Ira Dilworth, John Burnett, Roy Stibbs, Frank Levirs, Joe Phillipson, and Jim Carter had selectively scaled their way across the escarpments of educational leadership, navigating their ascent from the narrow world of local schools to district and regional prominence with the teachers' federation and, finally, to positions of importance in the provincial government, the highest educational stage of all until recent decades. Although clearly blessed with personal rewards, such individuals were generally heralded by the educational community—and by the public at large—for both their personal attainments and the great service they rendered to the provincial system along the way. For most, movement up the administrative ladder was often aided and abetted by the presence of an "old boys' network" that coached aspiring school leaders in the subtleties of induction processes and the rungs that were essential to climb.[71]

But ties within the world of schools were far more than "professional." Relations were often "familial" and "social" as much as anything else. A tradition of "teaching families" comprised of sisters, brothers, fathers and daughters, as well as husbands and wives, stretches back through the province's educational history to the Reverend and Mrs. Staines who taught the first HBC school, and to members of the Lawson, Glyde, and Young families who taught in Vancouver Island's first public schools.[72]

Social relationships also cemented the community together. Everyone, it appeared, knew someone who knew somebody else they knew. The degree of social and professional separation in public schooling was small, at times almost undetectable. In staff lunchrooms, professional get-togethers, conferences, and around educational campfires late at night, it was commonplace to hear: "I taught with the deputy minister's sister in Fort St. John," "I knew Dorothea at normal school before she became an inspector's wife." "Alex was my former principal," or "I remember professor so and so when he was a young teacher in Point Grey."[73] Such comments were frequently overheard at any educational gathering well into the 1970s.

This photograph included deputy minister Joe Phillipson (top centre) and his senior management committee (top right clockwise) Les Canty, C.I. Taylor, John Meredith, Bill Reid, Ed Espley, Andy Soles, and J.S. White.

Perhaps the greatest single example of the system's small social circumference can be seen in a 24" x 36" photograph of the deputy minister and seven members of the education department's management committee (overleaf). This photograph, reproduced on posterboard, graced the walls of school board and principals' offices around the province in the early 1970s and its significance lay in the fact that the officials were unidentified. The assumption was that everyone in the provincial system who "counted" already knew who these people were and additional identification was unnecessary.[74] In a minor act of rebellion, local educators and officials gleefully labelled the portrait of the system's senior management "Snow White and the Seven Dwarfs." But, on the downside, a world comprised of such close social relations between educators and bureaucrats—and that was small and comfortable in itself—was not entirely open to change and new ideas. This may, in part, explain the system's inherent conservatism and its defenselessness against the political forces that would soon overrun it.[75]

Schools Before Politics

Of course, the absence of politics—most notably partisan politics—made relationships easier. The educational world was generally unsullied by political intrigue until the 1960s and, in this regard, credit is due to the wisdom of politicians of all stripes who remained content to leave public education "out of politics" for best part of a century. Aside from the key position of superintendent of schools (after 1931 the deputy minister's position), an office where educators traditionally served "at the pleasure of the government," the education portfolio remained free of political influence. In attempting to recruit a senior educational civil servant in 1938, chief inspector H.B. King confidently wrote to an applicant: "with one exception nearly twenty years ago . . . educational positions have been regarded as outside politics."[76] The exception, of course, was Alexander Robinson who had served as superintendent of schools from 1899 to 1919 and whose tenure survived eight premiers and 16 ministers of education, until education minister J.D. MacLean took a personal dislike to the elegant and strong-minded Robinson and inserted his own candidate, Vancouver principal S.J. Willis. Generally speaking, the education department functioned throughout the first half of the twentieth century, in the words of a former inspector, as a "professional service" without much government interference. Even education ministers, for the most part, were no more than "nominal heads" of the civil service, a former inspector recalled.[77]

Earning a minister's displeasure did not necessarily prompt dismissal of a civil servant or, for that matter, the removal of a superintendent or a deputy minister. Incoming Social Credit education minister, Ray Williston, was mightily displeased with his deputy, Harold Campbell, who persistently thwarted his efforts in the mid-1950s to establish a second university in Victoria. Unbeknownst to Williston, Campbell had entered into a gentleman's agreement with UBC president, Norman McKenzie, that all new institutions would remain affiliated outposts of the province's first university.[78] Only when Williston was later redeployed as minister for lands was he able to outflank Campbell and secure property on which to build UVic. Such was the immense discretionary power of the educational mandarins. As late as 1971, senior bureaucrats claimed that the imperial age of school administration remained intact and refused to acknowledge that partisan politics were seeping into school government, or that the province's educational officers would ever witness educational decisions being shaped by the rough hands of politicians.[79]

A long tradition of civil service authority supported their view. Since the nineteenth century, British Columbians had come to accept that most teachers and educational civil servants were "small-l" liberals who were progressive minded in their views about schools and society. In an age that proclaimed the virtues of Liberalism writ large, this was not surprising. Little could be considered radical about the ideas of most educators who envisioned teaching as a "helping profession" and their work as an important part of social service.[80] Accordingly, the educational community was traditionally supportive of more and better schooling for everyone, the idea of children remaining in schools longer, the expansion of secondary schools into rural areas, and the provision of medical, dental, and nutritional services for youngsters and families in poor circumstances—in short, precisely the public school agenda sought by most people throughout the province in the nineteenth and twentieth centuries.

There were, certainly, a few exceptions. The Rural Teachers' Association (RTA) assumed a more militant posture during the Great Depression as rural teachers were galvanized into action by the wretched conditions of rural schools and rural life. Rightfully so, the RTA considered the BCTF's leadership as "an oligarchic dictatorship" dominated by urban concerns and blind to the hardships of poor country schools and the even poorer children who attended them.[81] Eventually, the RTA's influence raised the federation's consciousness about social justice and steered it toward affiliation with the Canadian labour movement before the end of World War II, the sole teachers' group in the country to be so aligned.[82]

On occasion, a few principals and teachers were also publicly active in politics but, on the whole, such behaviour was rare.[83] "Professional" and "union" interests remained generally well balanced in the teachers' federation before the end of the 1960s. As Charlie Ovans, the farsighted strategist who led the BCTF into the post-war era cogently warned his colleagues, reformers who "try to usurp the political function" of government "do not in the long run succeed."[84] All in all, for best part of a century, the province's educational cohort likely reflected in microcosm British Columbia's body politic, a bell-curve that straddled the ideological centre with a slight inclination to the left. Not surprisingly, Johnson's 1964 *History of Public Education in British Columbia*—a volume that remains the only full-length comprehensive historical study of provincial schools—made no mention of the word "politics" in either its 17-page chapter on the BCTF or in its general index.[85] Nor, indeed, did Johnson's broader treatment of the history of Canadian education mention "politics" when it appeared four years later.[86]

Educators look back on schools of the 1950s and 1960s as "happy kingdoms," comprised of parents, teachers, trustees, and the public, part of what former principal and, later, deputy minister R.J. "Jim" Carter summed up as "a kinder, gentler world" of provincial schooling.[87] Another principal, Duncan Lorimer at Victoria High, remembers asking teachers and being asked as a teacher himself, "Are you happy here?" following their appointments.[88]

In summary, from the beginning of the 1870s to the beginning of the 1970s, British Columbia's public school system, like the province as a whole, had largely remained "a world in itself," to borrow UBC historian Margaret Ormsby's description of British Columbia's historical tendency toward self-absorption.[89] For 100 years, schools had been governed and administered away from the public spotlight by a small educational bureau of government that was imperial in manner and unobtrusive in its practices. It was a system in which governance and administration were co-terminous, where information and problems flowed upward from local communities and decisions and solutions flowed downward from headquarters. For nearly a century, public education remained government's least visible and "quietest" portfolio by any measure.

All things considered, British Columbia's first century of schooling was spectacular in its attainments, given the challenges that geography, distance, and uneven settlement presented. Except for the lost decade of the Great Depression, the march toward a better educational future had proceeded steadily forward, supported by a great public consensus that all was right in the educational world and heaven and earth were properly aligned.[90] But for a brief *frisson* of alarm about the competitiveness of schools following the launching of the Soviet satellite, Sputnik, in 1957, public confidence in the system and public trust in teachers and educational officials remained high.[91] Educators and the public agreed. British Columbia had built a provincial school system that was admired, envied in fact, by other jurisdictions across the nation.[92]

However, the public school's immense success—and the great educational consensus it rested upon—would never be, as the *Daily Colonist* presciently reported in 1872, "acceptable to all and good enough for all."[93] From the 1870s to the 1950s, a modest number of so-called "private" schools continued to operate without any form of government inspection, mostly on Vancouver Island and in Vancouver's leafy groves, along with a small number of denominational schools dominated by the Catholic School Trustees' Association.

After war's end in 1945, however, non-public sector school growth became more vigorous and, between 1945 and 1978, 65 private schools were added, bringing the total size of this sector to 180 schools with an overall population of 24,000 pupils.[94] Backing for provincial support of non-public sector schools also increased in some quarters in a heady post-1945 climate of enthusiasm for all things educational. Former education minister in the progressive Liberal government of the wartime years (1941-1945), H.G.T. Perry, prompted discussion about "the problem of private schools" in a timely 1951 editorial that appeared in *The Prince Rupert Daily News*. "The art of high statesmanship," Perry advised, "is to so modify the will of the majority that the rights of minority groups are protected to such a degree that they . . . receive consideration and protection."[95] After pointing out the unfairness of a system in which property-owning parents of Catholic and other faiths "paid their school taxes to support the state public school system from which their children derive no benefit," Perry recommended appointing a royal commission to study the question and help the state resolve in educational terms how it might "realize and exercise its high responsibility of being fair and reasonable toward the claims of the minorities."[96]

Perry's advice was warmly received in a rights-conscious post-war world. In small ways after mid-century, provincial authorities began to respond to the notion that "double payment for both taxes and fees for educational services," as researchers for the 1988 royal commission on education would later put it, "was unjust and that choice of alternative forms of schooling constituted a democratic right befitting society as a whole."[97] In 1951, children in independent schools received free textbooks for the first time, and government shouldered the cost of children's dental and health services in Catholic parochial schools. Bus transportation for independent school youngsters was also provided through enabling legislation in the 1950s, although "not all school boards cooperated in sharing transportation facilities."[98] Schools in the non-public sector were also excused from municipal taxation in 1957 and, in 1967, another landmark development occurred when Notre Dame University, a Catholic institution in Nelson (now David Thompson University and a part of the post-secondary public system), received public funding. Taken as a whole, such events—together with the changing values of an increasingly diverse, open-minded, and pluralistic provincial society—helped foreshadow passage of Bill 33, the *School Support (Independent) Act* on March 30, 1977. Passage of the *Independent School Act* in 1989 recognized independent schools as an alternative to public schools for the first time and further extended financial support for non-public sector schools.[99]

Notes

1. Susan E. Houston, "Social Reform and Education: The Issue of Compulsory Schooling, Toronto 1851-71," in Neil McDonald and Alf Chaiton (Eds.), *Egerton Ryerson and His Times* (Toronto: Macmillan, 1978), 255.

2. Willard W. Waller, *The Sociology of Teaching* (New York: Wiley, 1932).

3. Marvin Lazerson, "Canadian Educational Historiography: Some Observations," in Neil McDonald and Alf Chaiton (Eds.), *Egerton Ryerson and His Times* (Toronto: Macmillan, 1978), 5.

4. Goldwin S. French, "Egerton Ryerson and the Methodist Model for Upper Canada," in Neil McDonald and Alf Chaiton (Eds.), *Egerton Ryerson and His Times*, (Toronto: Macmillan, 1978), 56.

5. Ibid.

6. As a social doctrine, liberalism came to embody a number of important philosophical ideas, including the assumptions: that individuals are perfectible through educational and social development; that social progress can be best assured through state planning and regulation; that social equality should be an important goal of state activity; that individuals and society should be organized according to rational and scientific paradigms in the interests of efficiency; that social welfare should be a government responsibility; and that social and individual differences are objectionable and should be minimized, if not eliminated, for the sake of social harmony.

7. G.M. Young, *Victorian England: Portrait of an Age* (London: Oxford University Press, 1960), 25.

8. Neil McDonald, "Egerton Ryerson and the School as an Agent of Political Socialization," in Neil McDonald and Alf Chaiton (Eds.), *Egerton Ryerson and His Times*, (Toronto: Macmillan, 1978), 98.

9. Young, *Victorian England*, 116.

10. Jean Barman, "Transfer, Imposition or Consensus? The Emergence of Educational Structures in Nineteenth-Century British Columbia," in Nancy M. Sheehan, J. Donald Wilson and David C. Jones (Eds.), *Schools in the West: Essays in Canadian Educational History* (Calgary: Detselig, 1986), 241.

11. Ibid., 242.

12. John Calam and Thomas Fleming, *British Columbia Schools and Society: Commissioned Papers, Volume 1* (Victoria: Queen's Printer, 1988), 54.

13. Barman, "Transfer, Imposition or Consensus," 243.

14. Ibid., 253.

15. Hubert Howe Bancroft, *History of British Columbia, 1792-1887: The Works of Hubert Howe Bancroft, Vol. XXXII* (San Francisco: The History Company, 1887), 735.

16. "The Opening of the Free Schools," *The British Colonist*, 2 August 1865, 2.

17. Calam and Fleming, *British Columbia Schools and Society*, 54.

18. Ibid.

19. L.W. Downey, "The Aid-to-Independent-Schools Movement in British Columbia," in Nancy M. Sheehan, J. Donald Wilson, and David C. Jones (Eds.), *Schools in the West: Essays in Canadian Educational History* (Calgary: Detselig, 1986), 306.

20. Ibid., 307.

21. Ibid., 305.

22. F. Henry Johnson, *A Brief History of Canadian Education* (Toronto: McGraw-Hill, 1968), 80. See also: F. Henry Johnson, *A History of Public Education in British Columbia* (Vancouver: University of British Columbia Publications Centre, 1964), 43-45.

23. Thomas Fleming, "In the Imperial Age and After: Patterns of British Columbia School Leadership and the Institution of the Superintendency, 1849-1988," in Thomas Fleming (Ed.), *School Leadership: Essays on the British Columbia Experience, 1872-1995* (Mill Bay, BC: Bendall Books, 2001), 164.

24. Houston, "Social Reform and Education," 255.

25. Lazerson, "Canadian Educational Historiography," 5.

26. Johnson, *A History of Public Education in British Columbia*, 56.

27. Johnson, *A Brief History*, 85.

28. Johnson, *A History of Public Education in British Columbia*, 56.

29. Rennie Warburton, "The Class Relations of Public School Teachers in British Columbia," *Canadian Review of Sociology and Anthropology*, Vol. 23, 2 (May 1986), 210-230. In this paper, Warburton describes teachers as dependent state employees.

30. Barman, "Transfer, Imposition or Consensus," 242.

31. *British Columbia, Annual Report of the Public Schools 1872-1873* (hereafter ARPS), 36. Jessop was an Englishman who emigrated to Ontario at the age of 17 where he likely worked first as a printer's apprentice before securing a teaching certificate at Ryerson's normal school in Toronto. A man of enormous physical energy, he elected to cross the continent on foot with a party of "overlanders," arriving in Victoria on New Year's Day 1860. After an ill-fated effort as principal of Victoria Central School, an endeavour that almost left him bankrupt, Jessop tried his hand at local and provincial politics to no avail. Important political connections, however, opened up new opportunities. A strong relationship with Rocke Robertson, provincial secretary for the first British Columbia government, led him to frame the first school act and to lobby successfully for the newly created superintendent of education's position.

32. Ibid., 6.

33. Ibid., 38. Getting into the province's interior was difficult at best in Jessop's day. On the mainland, wagon roads connected New Westminster with Fort Langley, the Dewdney Road linked Hope with Similakameen, and the Cariboo Road stretched from Yale to Soda Creek, where a steamer supplied passage to Quesnel. Otherwise, only the old fur brigade route spliced through the Okanagan Valley to Alexandria and some footpaths offered a small trail from the U.S. border to the foothills of the Rockies. From Victoria, New Westminster was accessible by steamboat, as was Port Townsend, Comox and, sometimes, Skeena. Sternwheelers afforded water transportation from New Westminster to Yale. Until 1885, however, when the Canadian Pacific Railroad reached Port Moody from Eastern Canada, much of the province's vast hinterland was more easily reached from the U.S. than from the province's capital city. The Northern Pacific Railway ran between Minneapolis and Seattle with a stop in Northern Idaho 34 miles from Bonners' Ferry that was connected by the Kootenai River to Creston, from which other interior B.C. settlements could be reached.

34. Thomas Fleming and Helen Raptis, "Government's Paper Empire: Historical Perspectives on Measuring Student Achievement in British Columbia Schools, 1872-1999," *Journal of Educational Administration and History*, Vol. 37, No. 2 (September 2005), 183.

35. Ibid.

36. With minimal clerical and professional assistance, superintendent of education Alexander Robinson (1899-1919) managed much of the provincial school system single-handedly, even when acting simultaneously as the province's public service commissioner. Such was the reach and the control of senior officials. For a discussion of Robinson's stewardship, see Thomas Fleming, "Letters from Headquarters: Alexander Robinson and the British Columbia Education Office, 1899-1919," in Thomas Fleming (Ed.), *School Leadership: Essays on the British Columbia Experience, 1872-1995* (Mill Bay, BC: Bendall Books, 2001), 18-53.

37. Jean Barman, *The West Beyond the West* (Toronto: University of Toronto Press, 1991).

38. British Columbia Department of Education, *One Hundred Years: Education in British Columbia*, (Victoria: Queen's Printer, 1972), 74.

39. William Bruneau, "'Still Pleased to Teach:' A Thematic Study of the British Columbia Teachers' Federation, 1917-1978," Unpublished paper, University of British Columbia, 1978, 35.

40. Roth Garthley Gordon, "Secondary Education in Rural British Columbia," Unpublished master's thesis, Department of Philosophy, University of British Columbia, 1935. 43, 123, and 174.

41. Leslie Dyson and Chuck Gosbee, *Glancing Back: Reflections and Anecdotes on Vancouver Public Schools*, (Vancouver: Vancouver School Board, 1988), 71.

42. Board of School Trustees of the City of Vancouver, *Educational Institutions of Vancouver* (Vancouver: Board of School Trustees, 1910), 9.

43. Johnson, *A History of Public Education in British Columbia*, 70.

44. Interview with Wilf Graham, Chilliwack, 11 October 1989.

45. Interviews with Bernard Gillie, Victoria, 3 November 1988, and 16 November 1988.

46. British Columbia Department of Education, *One Hundred Years: Education in British Columbia*, 82. Even today, it remains questionable if more than four out of five students complete all their high school coursework. Recent analysis suggests that high school completion rates for male students in British Columbia are 75 per cent and 83 per cent for male and female students respectively. See British Columbia Ministry of Education, 2008-2009 *Summary of Key Information*, retrieved 20 December 2010 from www.bced. gov.bc.ca/keyinfo/pdfs/ski09/pdf, 56.

47. Except for a few well-publicized spats between the Vancouver school board and, to a far lesser extent, the Victoria school board during the first two decades of the twentieth century over demands for local autonomy, little evidence of conflict between provincial and local authorities can be found until the 1960s.

48. Fleming, "Letters From Headquarters," 36.

49. Ibid. 32-46.

50. Ibid.

51. The ongoing cooperative character of the relationship between government and the trustees could be seen in government's 1958 decision to close the school inspectorate and to establish greater levels of local control through district-based superintendents. This move was favoured by many districts and by the BCSTA in general.

52. James B. London, *Public Education Public Pride: The Centennial History of the British Columbia School Trustees Association* (Vancouver: British Columbia School Trustees Association, 2005), 207.

53. Thomas Fleming, "'Our Boys in the Field:' School Inspectors, Superintendents, and the Changing Character of School Leadership in British Columbia," in Thomas Fleming (Ed.), *School Leadership: Essays on the British Columbia Experience, 1872-1995* (Mill Bay, BC: Bendall Books, 2001), 60.

54. John Calam, *Alex Lord's British Columbia: Recollections of a Rural School Inspector, 1915-1936* (Vancouver: University of British Columbia Press, 1991).

55. Ibid., 36.

56. Ibid., 9-10; see also Thomas Fleming, *The Principal's Office and Beyond: Volume 1, Public School Leadership in British Columbia, 1849-2005* (Calgary: Detselig, 2010), 113-116.

57. ARPS 1888-1889, 216.

58. ARPS 1894-1895, 252.

59. ARPS 1896-1897, 238.

60. This is well documented in assorted essays found in Jean Barman, Neil Sutherland, and J.D. Wilson (Eds.), *Children, Teachers and Schools in the History of British Columbia* (Calgary: Detselig, 1995).

61. Interviews with Bernard Gillie, Victoria, 3 November 1988 and 16 November 1988.

62. Interviews with Stewart Graham, Burnaby, 18 and 19 December 1988.

63. Interviews with Bernard Gillie, Victoria, 3 November 1988 and 16 November 1988.

64. British Columbia Department of Education, *One Hundred Years*, 70.

65. Ibid.

66. Bruneau, "'Still Pleased to Teach,'" 9.

67. Ibid.

68. See Johnson, *A History of Public Education in British Columbia*, 254; and, Thomas Fleming, "A Compendium of British Columbia Principals for Select Years, 1872-1975," available electronically at: www.viu.ca/homeroom/principals.htm.

69. Bruneau, "'Still Pleased to Teach,'" 10.

70. Interviews with Stewart Graham, Burnaby, 18 and 19 December 1988.

71. Traditions of recruitment are described in Fleming, "'Our Boys in the Field:' School Inspectors, Superintendents, and the Changing Character of School Leadership in British Columbia," 61-65.

72. Thomas Fleming, "British Columbia Principals: Scholar-Teachers and Administrative Amateurs in Victorian and Edwardian Eras, 1872-1918," in Thomas Fleming (Ed.), *School Leadership: Essays on the British Columbia Experience, 1872-1995* (Mill Bay, BC: Bendall Books, 2001), 259.

73. For descriptions of historical relationships among educators, government, trustees, and the public in British Columbia, see Fleming, *The Principal's Office and Beyond, Volume 1*, 54-55, 79-80, 85-88, and 108-120.

74. I am indebted to former superintendent, Bob Overgaard, for pointing out the significance of the photograph without the names appended.

75. Barry Anderson brought this point to my attention after reading an early draft of this manuscript.

76. Thomas Fleming and David Conway, "Setting Standards in the West: C.B. Conway, Science, and School Reform in British Columbia, 1938-1974," in Thomas Fleming (Ed.), *School Leadership: Essays on the British Columbia Experience, 1872-1995* (Mill Bay, BC: Bendall Books, 2001), 137.

77. Interview with Wilf Graham, Chilliwack, 11 October 1989.

78. Colin Chasteneuf, "Interview with R.B. Williston, Minister of Education 1954-1956," 28 January 1993, Unpublished paper, University of Victoria.

79. Interview with Joe Phillipson, Victoria, 28 October 1983.

80. Dan C. Lortie, *Schoolteacher: A Sociological Study* (Chicago: University of Chicago Press, 1975), 28-29.

81. For the hardships of rural teachers' lives in the decades between the wars, see: J. D. Wilson, "'I am ready to be of assistance when I can': Lottie Bowron and the Rural Women Teachers in British Columbia," in Jean Barman, Neil Sutherland, and J. D. Wilson (Eds.), *Children, Teachers and Schools in the History of British Columbia* (Calgary: Detselig, 1995), 285-306; Thomas Fleming, Carolyn Smyly, and Julie White, "Beyond Hope and Past Redemption: Lottie Bowron and the Rural School Teachers of British Columbia, 1928-1934" in Thomas Fleming (Ed.), *School Leadership: Essays on the British Columbia Experience, 1872-1995* (Mill Bay, BC: Bendall Books, 2001), 101-132; and Thomas Fleming, and Carolyn Smyly, "The Diary of Mary Williams: A Cameo of Rural Schooling in British Columbia, 1922-1924" in Thomas Fleming (Ed.), *School Leadership: Essays on the British Columbia Experience, 1872-1995* (Mill Bay, BC: Bendall Books, 2001), 369-403.

82. F. Henry Johnson, "V. Revolt: The RTA in British Columbia," 236-272, in "A History of Public Education in British Columbia Amended Manuscript," University of British Columbia Special Collections, 239.

83. A few political activists of note were Arnold Webster, principal of Vancouver's Magee High, and his schoolteacher wife, Daisy de Jong. In 1953, Webster succeeded CCF party leader Harold Winch and served a term as leader of the opposition in the provincial legislature before retiring from politics. Miss de Jong, was a teacher who became a government inspector of home economics classes, was also politically involved, working on behalf of the CCF and, later, the NDP in the 1950s and 1960s. See Daisy Webster, "The Challenges of Home Economics," *THESA Journal*, Vol. 11, No. 1 (1973), 2-5. http://bctf.ca/thesa/pdf/Vol11_1Webster.pdf, retrieved 12 December 2009. Mount View High School principal Dr. J.M. Thomas, also stood for office as a CCF candidate in the 1950s.

84. Charlie Ovans, "The School System and School Administration: Past, Present and Future," *Eighth Annual Conference of the British Columbia Principals' and Vice-Principals' Association, 13-16 October 1976, Powell River, B.C.*, 40.

85. Johnson, *A History of Public Education in British Columbia*, 237-254 and 278.

86. Johnson, *A Brief History*, 213.

87. Interview with R.J. Carter, Vancouver, 28 May 1998.

88. Interview with Duncan Lorimer, Victoria, 12 May 1998.

89. Margaret Ormsby, *British Columbia: A History* (Vancouver: Macmillan, 1958), 491 and 494.

90. During the Depression, enrollments and spending declined. See British Columbia Department of Education, *One Hundred Years*, 68 and 80.

91. Sputnik's educational effects in provincial schools are discussed in Tara Toutant, "'Whoever has knowledge has the future at his feet:' The Canadian Educational Response to the Sputnik Crisis," Unpublished paper, University of Victoria, April 1993.

92. From the time Alexander Robinson came west to serve as principal of Vancouver High in 1892, British Columbia became known across the nation for the prominence of its educators and the quality of the provincial system. Figures such as George Weir, H.B. King, S.J. Willis, Robert Straight, Max Cameron, and C.B. Conway, to name but a few, surrounded the province in educational glory as educational administrators, organizers, and thinkers. Conway's prominence in the testing and measurement community is documented in Fleming and Conway, "Setting Standards in the West," 133-158.

93. Barman, "Transfer, Imposition or Consensus," 253.

94. The post-1945 growth of independent, Catholic, and other denominational schools is chronicled in Victoria Cunningham, *Justice Achieved: The Political Struggle of Independent Schools in British Columbia* (Vancouver: FISA, 2002).

95. *The Prince Rupert Daily News*, "The Problem of Private Schools," Tuesday 23 October 1951, 2. Harry G.T. Perry was managing editor of the newspaper.

96. Ibid.

97. Calam and Fleming, *British Columbia Schools and Society: Commissioned Papers, Volume 1*, 54.

98. Ibid.

99. The revitalization of non-public sector schools in the mid-twentieth century was examined also in Downey's essay, "The Aid-to-Independent-Schools Movement in British Columbia," cited earlier.

IMAGES:

Rural Schools and Rural Life

Modest in size but not in importance, even small communities tried to build the best schools they could afford. Here, young girls stand before the first school at Box Lake in the Central Kootenay region in the 1880s. Courtesy British Columbia Archives B-02657.

Riding to school was common in the late-nineteenth and early-twentieth centuries when long distances to rural schools were hard for children to manage on foot, or roads were poor. Here mounted children stand before Round Prairie School in the Thompson-Nicola region (ca. 1900). **Courtesy British Columbia Archives F-0220.**

The public or "common" school's mandate to "educate everyone" meant children from all families, rich and poor, attended. This photograph of a teacher and youngsters in a rural school (ca. 1900) illustrates that some youngsters walked to school without shoes. In British Columbia's poorest regions, children without shoes could be found attending school well into the Depression years of the 1930s. **Courtesy City of Vancouver Archives CVA-Sch-P99.**

Few rural schools were characterized by elegant design or permanent building materials. The broken windows and rough school yard that characterized North Arm School in 1907 (Moberly School) testified to the sometimes harsh realities of country life and to the wear and tear exacted on schools from rambunctious pupils of different ages and sizes.
Courtesy City of Vancouver Archives CVA-Sch-P149.

The last class at Craigflower School, the province's oldest surviving schoolhouse, located outside Victoria. Craigflower was established as the Maple Point School at the Hudson's Bay Craigflower Farm in 1855 to meet the educational needs of the children of farm employees and those of arriving settlers. This photograph shows the class of 1911, the final class to be instructed in the original building. **Courtesy British Columbia Archives G-02294.**

Even in rural schools, teachers tried to instill a sense of order and decorum in children as youngsters file into the first Cherry Creek School, situated in the Thompson-Nicola region, in 1918. **Courtesy British Columbia Archives C-08034.**

Schoolhouses were central to community life across the province, especially in remote settlements such as Atlin in British Columbia's northern Stikine region. More than just centres of learning, plain but sturdy schoolhouses like this one routinely served as the community's only centre for public events, civic meetings, dances, as well as musical and dramatic presentations. Here youngsters are shown leaving school for the day in 1921.
Courtesy British Columbia Archives G-06404.

Schools such as these were common across British Columbia and, indeed, the western provinces generally before the end of World War II, though few were as beautifully sited as this school in the Rockies, 1940. **Courtesy City of Vancouver Archives CVA-586-293.**

A time before support staff in schools. Pupils in the Rhone School in the Kootenay-Boundary region in 1945 at work scraping, sanding, and painting. **Courtesy British Columbia Archives I-00528.**

When everyone was expected to help. Older pupils at Westbank School in the Okanagan Valley serve cocoa to younger ones in 1945. Courtesy British Columbia Archives I-00518.

School clubs were immensely popular in the period between the wars and after. The boys' cooking club is at work here in Phillip Sheffield High School in the Central Fraser Valley in 1946. Courtesy British Columbia Archives I-00517.

World War II's end ushered in a floodtide of changes to society and schools. A "baby boom" prompted skyrocketing enrollments and unprecedented school building programs throughout the 1950s and 1960s. With land relatively cheap in booming towns and cities across British Columbia, hundreds of new schools appeared, many of them single-storey and "horizontal" constructions emblematic of the new international style. This Boston Bar school was photographed in 1960. **Courtesy British Columbia Archives I-23817.**

Well into the middle of the twentieth century and beyond, one-room schools could still be found scattered across isolated British Columbia communities. One such school was Topley School in the Buckley-Nechako region, photographed here amid a winter landscape in 1957.
Courtesy British Columbia Archives C-07871

A teacher and youngsters at the Tatlayoko School in the Cariboo in 1951. This was the kind of one-room school with limited educational programs and sparse resources that educational reformers sought to consolidate after 1945 into larger schools and larger school districts with larger tax bases. **Courtesy British Columbia Archives I-31890.**

CHAPTER 2

From Unity to Discord

Government's *1971-1972 Annual Report* on the schools provided little indication that the future of public schooling in British Columbia would differ much from the past.[1] Certainly, it offered no suggestion of deep fissures in the educational fabric that would tear apart schools in the years ahead, nor did it give any indication that the institution of public education in future decades would be anything other than what it had been for the past 100 years—dependable in its operations, understandable in its behaviours, harmonious in its parts, and purposeful in its objectives.

Much of the report offered a gentle and impressionistic sketch of an archaic educational world slipping further into the mists of the past. Only 93 of the one-room schools that had characterized provincial education for a century remained, down appreciably in number from the 233 that existed in the early 1960s.[2] Still, a few coastal school districts continued to employ a handful of old fashioned water taxis to ferry youngsters to schools between offshore islands, or back and forth along remote stretches of the foreshore as they had done for years. And, harkening back to early post-war years, some 500 secondary pupils from districts still without senior schools were living in dormitories in other and more fortunate districts, where they were enjoying a $40-a-month boarding allowance while completing their studies. Relations with teachers and trustees were sound, the report also advised in off-the-cuff fashion, and noted modestly the ease of articulation among the operations of schools, colleges, and universities.

By today's standards, some things were conspicuous by their absence. The report made no mention of English as a second language (ESL), or of other language and cultural issues. Nor did it refer to the galaxy of remedial programs and services that would transform the face of schools in the days immediately ahead. Nothing in the report's pages suggested an educational world on the verge of momentous change, nor did it disclose developments on the horizon that might reshape the face of the public schools, or destroy the state of social relations in the educational community— particularly those between government and the teachers' federation. From the vantage point of educational government, everything was fine with the schools.

District Consolidation's Dysfunctional Effects

But changes were already underway that would soon shake the very foundations of provincial schooling and the professional lives of those who managed and worked in it. One of the most important of these changes was prompted by government itself and could be traced back 25 years. This was the school consolidation movement that provincial authorities implemented in 1946, following UBC professor Max Cameron's inquiry into the state of school finance.[3] War's end had ushered in a time of exhilarating growth and prosperity and raised new questions about how to fulfill the promise of making secondary schooling available to everyone, a promise largely deferred by the Great Depression and World War II. The Depression, in particular, had underscored the grave disparities in educational opportunities available to children in urban and rural schools and had prompted government to commission Cameron's study. School governance and finance, Cameron found, were in a shambles in many small districts. In 1944, the province's 650 school districts were governed by 437 school boards and 213 government-appointed official trustees.[4] Making matters more complicated was the fact that 590 of these districts were rural and, altogether, enrolled no more than 23,000, or slightly less than 20 per cent, of the approximately 125,000 youngsters then enrolled in provincial schools.[5]

Cameron confirmed what was already well known—namely that many of the province's small rural districts were inefficient and too small in size to provide a tax base capable of sustaining secondary schools.[6] They were also grossly over-administered. In many instances, three trustees with scant educational knowledge or interest hired, fired, and supervised the district's educational work, usually carried out by one teacher in one school.[7] The inequity of such relationships were forever etched in the Canadian consciousness in Robert Harris' revealing 1885 painting, "The Meeting of the School Trustees," in which young teacher Kate Henderson appears to be explaining herself to four stern-faced men on a Prince Edward Island school board.

"Costs per pupil still vary so widely as to indicate great differences in the quality of the schooling provided," Cameron reported, advising further that "differences in ability to pay for education, and in the burden of school taxes, are undoubtedly substantial." British Columbia's immense geography, however, precluded the elimination of all differences. "Nature, with an irritating disregard for the problem of school administration," wrote Cameron, "has decreed that no system will produce perfect equality."[8] Nevertheless, he counselled, existing inequalities could be reduced through a massive amalgamation plan that would greatly enlarge the size of the districts that remained.[9]

Cameron's recommendations were fast-tracked and translated into 1946 legislation with far-reaching effects. Following a year of planning and consultation on the part of the education department, some 650 provincial school districts were reorganized in 1947 into 89 districts and, in 1971, reduced further to 74.[10] Consolidation proved enormously effective in alleviating many of the fiscal inequities that dogged provincial schools since Jessop's days. Most importantly, it led government to impose a standard assessment rate to be levied on property for educational purposes. Provincial grants were distributed at disproportionately high rates to comparatively poor districts in order to guarantee the availability of a basic educational program everywhere in the province. Permitting school boards to levy additional taxes to supplement the basic education program preserved local autonomy and initiative.

In addition, by consolidating districts into larger geographic units with greater numbers of people, school populations were amassed in sizes large enough to support secondary schools. Occasionally, the amalgamation of small districts produced as many problems as solutions. Assigned to the Stikine region, administrators found themselves in charge of an educational dominion "larger than France," where schools were scattered over a vast territory that could only be crossed in one day by plane.[11]

In its enthusiasm for educational equity and a more effective tax regime, government failed to contemplate consolidation's other effects, most notably its impact on school boards, and the social and political strains that amalgamation would provoke between provincial and local authorities. Instead of safeguarding budgets of hundreds of dollars, as they historically did, post-war boards began to oversee budgets of millions of dollars for local schools scattered across broader and more diverse jurisdictions. Board autonomy was also enlarged in several respects after mid-century as the province relaxed some regulations, allowing trustees greater influence in shaping parts of the educational program. Taxation powers also enabled boards to shape school districts' identities through particular capital construction projects.

Consolidation likewise transformed the BCSTA in the post-war era into a powerful and increasingly sophisticated organization—something it had never been since its establishment. "For the first 50 years of its existence," historian James London observed, "the BCSTA was embryonic . . . more concerned with its survival than with expanding its operations."[12] But consolidation changed all this by equipping trustees with a far larger political base from which to assert their independence and to pitch their claims for greater control over educational policy. By the mid-1950s, trustees and their association were warming up to do battle with provincial authorities on a variety of fronts, pressing wherever they could for greater district autonomy.

Local control of administrative appointments quickly emerged as a key objective for trustees. The story was simple: in the transition to larger units of governance, trustees found themselves relying on inspectors to execute local administrative tasks in addition to the supervisory and reporting chores they were already carrying out on behalf of government. With the establishment of 74 large districts, in effect, each inspector became the *de facto* general superintendent for one or more local systems. However, the idea of granting trustees local control of administrative appointments was a deep-rooted and thorny issue.[13]

Throughout the twentieth century, government had steadfastly maintained its influence over local administration through the appointment of municipal and rural inspectors. Trustees were rebuffed in the early 1950s when the BCSTA proposed to shift control over senior administrative appointments to local boards, arguing essentially that Cameron's 1946 restructuring had given trustees greater responsibilities for district schools but had done nothing to increase district authority in educational matters, particularly with respect to selecting their own school leaders.[14] Again, the province refused. However, the province did concede some important ground by closing the school inspectorate in 1958 and by creating the office of district superintendent—a position whose costs were jointly underwritten by provincial and local authorities.

Not satisfied with this change, the BCSTA, as well as the BCTF, lobbied more forcefully for decentralizing educational authority in their 1958 submissions to the Chant royal commission, a commission occasioned by Sputnik and fears of Soviet educational supremacy, especially in mathematics and the sciences. The BCSTA advised Chant that a district superintendent must be "closely identified with the school system," and that each board must therefore "be permitted to appoint its own superintendent . . . whose line of authority would emanate from the school board."[15] Chant listened but government did nothing to change matters when the commission's report was tabled in 1960.

The idea of local employment, however, was kept alive by events inside the civil service. The department's officers, first the inspectors and, after 1958, the district superintendents, felt aggrieved because of the low salaries they received. This was a historical problem that dated back to Robinson's reign as school chief (1899-1919) and that surfaced repeatedly in the decades since.[16] Each time the complaint was the same and each time the issue was unresolved—the civil service "salary tree" could not be shaken. Particularly galling was the fact that high school and urban principals were routinely paid far higher salaries than inspectors or superintendents, even though principals were ranked lower in the province's administrative hierarchy—an anomaly condemned in 1925 by school commissioners Putman and Weir and, in 1960, by Chant.[17]

Calls to grant school districts autonomy over senior administrative appointments continued to be ignored throughout W.A.C. Bennett's Social Credit administrations in the 1960s and early 1970s. Bennett, an avowed centralist, was unwilling to expand district control over education. Although the BCSTA and the BCTF often pursued separate ambitions, the two organizations occasionally presented a united front to government after mid-century, especially on issues to do with decentralizing educational authority and increasing district budgets.[18]

Bennett's political passing in 1972 pushed local control onto the front tables of government, abetted by the new government's commitment to relocate educational decision making "out there, among the people," as one senior civil servant of the day described it.[19] Among other things, Dave Barrett's NDP government heralded the virtues of decentralization and, accordingly, districts with an enrollment of 20,000 pupils were granted the right to hire their own superintendents on April 18, 1973. The first major engagement in the 70-year struggle for local control was over. On August 12, 1980, the larger struggle was won when Bill Bennett's Social Credit government consented to give school districts of all sizes authority to appoint their own chief school officers. Frustrated with low civil service salaries, and captivated by generous remuneration packages offered by school boards, the government's men jumped ship leaving the field services division—and government's influence over local school management—a shell of its former self.

Local employment of district superintendents changed the entire alignment of the educational universe. On the surface, it simply meant a change in the allegiance of district superintendents from provincial authorities to their new political masters on school boards. But, more importantly, it represented a fundamental separation of legislative and administrative authority—two elements of governance that had remained unified for more than 100 years. This separation meant more than the end of imperial administrative traditions. It bespoke a fundamental disconnection at the core of public education's administrative structure. From now on, the people who would make the rules—and shape government's legislative agenda—would be distinct from the people who implemented the legislation and regulations in local schools.

This change also meant that district-appointed leaders would no longer be able to influence government policies and priorities through first-hand knowledge of local schools and communities. In opting for local employment—and ending their relationship with the education department—superintendents also severed their access to the inside political and economic understandings they traditionally enjoyed as government's men. Without such intelligence, superintendents' lives became far more existential in character. No longer would "headquarters" supply them with advance particulars or background about what government in Victoria planned to do and why.

The departure of district superintendents from government likewise ensured that a new chapter in school management would be more adversarial in character. As standard bearers for individual districts, superintendents were now naturally obliged to compete with each other—and do battle with provincial authorities—for their district's share of public school budgets. In a new and more competitive climate, feelings of mutual trust and cooperation evaporated, along with the informality and confidentiality that were historically the hallmarks of school board relations with the education office. Missing also was the geniality and camaraderie that once bound together the government's "boys in the field." From this time on, agreements were no longer sealed in handshakes and tacit understandings. Such antiquated gestures appeared insufficient and were now discarded as a century-old model of government-by-men gave way to a model of government-by-laws.[20]

Local employment also meant district school leaders were suddenly exposed to changeable local politics with no government help or protection. And turbulent their lives soon proved to be. Within a decade of local employment, 67 of the 129 men and women who served as chief educational officers for the province's 75 school districts left or were dismissed from superintendencies in British Columbia.[21] District leadership, in fact, had not simply shifted from provincial to district officers within professional ranks, it had also passed from professional and provincial ranks directly into the hands of district trustees, who now enjoyed full and unprecedented authority over their own locally selected and "paid for" superintendents. For better or worse, educational decision making had moved from government's dignified halls into the boisterous precincts of local affairs where issues were customarily parochial in scope, blunt in definition, and subject to immediate political timetables. The days when patient and farsighted school mandarins could confidentially consider the fate of local schools, and how government could assist them, were over. A century of unrevealed give and take had produced a discreet culture of quiet agreement between local districts and the government's school bureau: this was about to give way to a new and much louder culture of discontent and complaint.

Local employment proved equally costly to educational government. After 1980, the educational civil service increasingly found itself divorced from "the real world of the schools," as practitioners put it, sadly missing the close relationships, vital information, subtle grasp of events, and common sense that government school inspectors and superintendents "in the field" had supplied for nearly a century.

To be sure, other negative effects of school consolidation deserve mention, not the least of which was the system-wide bureaucracy that district amalgamation and local control of administrative appointments unintentionally produced. Prior to 1946, bureaucratization was unknown in most of the province's 650 school districts, except in Vancouver, Victoria, New Westminster, and Nanaimo where specialized management functions had evolved in city systems to service swelling school populations. But, elsewhere, the only permanent "official" or "bureaucratic" presence in most districts was the local high school, or elementary, principal who served as the board's educational confidant and advised the district secretary between a school inspector's annual or bi-annual visits.

However, the advent of sizeable school territories, grander schools, substantial staffs, and the post-1945 move to comprehensive high school education, forced district administrations to expand their operational scope, and to develop specialized structures for the many responsibilities schools were now bearing—in effect, to bureaucratize. This process carried its own by-products: typically, changes in size and structure formalized relations between district offices and government; between district offices and their staffs; and between school districts, schools, and the families they served.[22] Bureaucratization meant that rules, regulations, and policies now prescribed behaviour—rather than experience or inter-personal relations—not just at the provincial level but now, too, at district and school levels. By creating larger governance units and more powerful school boards, consolidation also inadvertently created larger and more powerful local bargaining units for teachers and, also, formalized relations between teachers' locals and district offices. It also increased the social distance between administrators and teachers—and between teachers and the community. In large districts, this proved problematic in another way since money was perceived to come from "government" with no related cost to local taxpayers.

In summary, by changing the territorial scale of school governance and administration across the province, consolidation created new and larger organizational structures unanticipated in early school legislation or in the traditions that subsequently evolved to manage and direct provincial schools. These included powerful teacher bargaining units at the district level, school district bureaucracies, a more ambitious provincial trustee association, and superintendents' offices "owned and operated" by local trustees. Put another way, Cameron's plan for consolidation led to the creation of structures, organizations, and relationships that were never a part of British Columbia's earlier school history. The impact that these new structures and organizations would have on provincial schooling in the second half of the twentieth century— especially on governance, management, and labour relations—would prove profound. Although district consolidation had brought forth a school system undoubtedly more equitable in educational and, especially, fiscal terms, it was not without costs. It had unwittingly set into motion a train of events that gave rise to adversarial governance, administrative, and labour structures which would greatly dissolve the cooperative and harmonious relations that characterized the educational community before 1946.

Drift and Disappearance in Educational Government

A second development that would transform the state of provincial schools after 1972 and contribute to schooling's haunted condition was the decline and fall of educational government.[23] Even before the 1960s drew to a close, it was apparent the old order of school governance and administration in British Columbia was unravelling. By the late 1960s, the education department had become an aging unit of government that had done little to renew itself since 1945. It had, in effect, become a "closed shop" where older officers selected younger officers much like themselves—and where advancement increasingly became a matter of "waiting one's turn." With scant guidance from ministers, and little supervision from the deputy's office, the department operated for much of the time without an explicit agenda, save for "more of the same." Only the "colleges and universities" branch of the civil service had really prospered after mid-century with the establishment of two new universities and a go-ahead community college plan.[24] But, otherwise, this centralized and sedate world of provincial school administration was disintegrating as the 1960s turned into the 1970s, corroded from within by the maintenance of outdated traditions and harassed from without by powerful new forces that few in government understood.

Other factors were also hastening the demise of the established administrative order. The "baby boom" that started in 1946, together with huge increases in secondary school participation after 1945, turned the spotlight of public attention on the schools. By 1971, one out of four British Columbians was in school, making the public school the province's most important educational institution, as well as an instrumental plank in government's overall public policy.[25] An even more significant factor in raising education's public profile was the skyrocketing level of funding it demanded. Capital expenditures on provincial schooling soared from some $17 million in 1960 to nearly $67 million in 1974, an increase of nearly 300 per cent.[26] Operating expenditures for school boards likewise rose sharply over the same period, leaping from about $100 million to nearly $530 million, an increase of 416 per cent which prompted considerable public alarm.[27]

The NDP's election in 1972 made matters worse for an education department already surrendering its influence to politicians.[28] The new government's distrust of its own educational civil service was soon made apparent when education minister, former teacher, and Burnaby school trustee, Eileen Dailly, moved aside the department's senior staff in favour of outside appointments and overturned longstanding traditions that had vested authority in the civil service and district superintendents. The system would be refocused, Dailly warned, around "the teacher, the parent, and the child" not "the superintendent, the principal, and the teacher," as it was in the past.[29]

Dailly's attempts to "democratize" the public system were fraught with miscues and misadventures. Aimless excursions around the province by commissioner John Bremer, her lead hand in reform, precipitated his dismissal by the premier and cost the minister a severe loss of political face. Dailly's next initiative, the establishment of a new "research and development division," headed by former UBC quarterback-turned-pedagogical-expert Stanley Knight proved no less problematic. Recruited "to assist in the development of changes in education," Knight and the "R and D" group's overtly political agenda brought them into open conflict with the department's old guard, forcing Dailly to suspend the newcomers' operations. Even the BCTF, who had vigorously endorsed her, appeared stunned by her maladroitness and, before the end of 1975, an ebbing economic tide would dispatch the reform-happy NDP government.

The challenges facing educational government for the next decade and a half would prove far more difficult than shoring up a minister's shortcomings. The 1960s, among other things, had greatly reshaped the contours of

Canadian society and changed women's status and their place in the nation's economic and social life.[30] A revolution in family life (some called it a "breakdown"), shifting immigration patterns, new language and cultural policies, as well as the influx of diverse pupil populations, imposed new social responsibilities on schools and created a broader and more difficult agenda for educational government.

By the mid-1970s, the education department seemed overcome by events swirling around government. On one side, it found itself obliged to respond to an array of equity and access issues raised by long-neglected and disenfranchised constituencies who now saw fit to challenge the fairness of schools and their responsiveness to handicapped or "special needs" children.[31] These and other constituencies—including women and various ethnic and minority groups—pressed government hard to provide integration for handicapped learners, to improve social and medical services, and to introduce curricular reform and non-sexist literature in schools. Driving the movement to enlarge the school's ambit was a constellation of special interest groups—including the teachers' federation, of course—insisting it was imperative for schools to extend their reach farther into the social domain because the foundations of family life had changed.

Almost always, requests for new programs and services were couched in principles of equity and social justice. Advocates of various causes argued that past social, educational, and economic inequities could only be addressed by forceful public initiatives to reduce social and individual differences. As public institutions, schools were deemed ideal agencies for such a crusade: they offered direct, convenient, systematic, and efficient points of contact with children and their families. Moreover, the school's historical mission to ensure educational equity could simply be extended to include social equity. In less than a decade, such reasoning helped convert the public school from an agency whose historical mission was primarily educational in character to an agency charged with both educational and social functions. Any resistance by government leaders to this new mission was drowned by a chorus of voices, each proclaiming to hold a special warrant to speak on behalf of children's educational or social needs.

Educational bureaucrats soon found themselves overwhelmed by a barrage of requests for additional resources. Many of the problems they faced could be traced to the fact that the demands being made were unprecedented in both kind and number. School government had never before processed these kinds of input: this was not the way the educational civil service operated. Government had always written its own script for the schools, defining its purposes, directions, and priorities. But now no agenda was discernable. Not really knowing what to do—and not really being able to calculate the political consequences of saying no—government mindlessly acceded to most demands and, in so doing, allowed special interest constituencies to rewrite the school's mandate.[31] This was a landmark event. It signified the first time in provincial school history that an education bureau had allowed individuals and organizations outside government to determine what schools would actually do.

Making matters worse was the fact that this change effectively reduced provincial authorities to the role of paymaster, picking up the tab for programs and services commissioned by others. This proved costly. Between the school years 1944-1945 and 1971-1972, the provincial government spent almost twice the amount school districts spent on schools. Moreover, throughout much of the 1970s, the province seemed incapable of slowing spending. For example, the education ministry's budget estimates jumped 36 per cent from $553 million in 1975 to $754 million in 1976.[32] Across a three-year period in the mid-1970s, the teaching force climbed 21 per cent while the school population increased only two per cent.[33] Even more disturbing was the realization that the education ministry had insufficient fiscal controls to track how these large outflows of provincial money were being allocated, or to ascertain if these monies were well spent.[34] Accounting procedures in educational government, as one incoming deputy found, were a mess.[35]

While government was attempting to address this clamour for a new mandate and a broader, fairer, and more "inclusionary" concept of schooling, it was also besieged by demands for other kinds of accountability to do with slowing annual increases in school expenditures and improving academic performance. Concerns with lack of educational quality and focus emerged in the early 1970s in reaction to "looser" curricular requirements and "softer" school standards introduced a decade earlier. By the mid-1970s, fears about declining scholastic scores in schools blazed across news headlines and editorial pages in the province's popular press, reflecting a burgeoning unease about educational performance and student behaviour, especially in secondary schools.[36] Unmoved by government promises to improve accountability, parents and community leaders demanded more substantial evidence about how well youngsters could read, write, and add.[37] Such criticisms and demands pulled educational discussions out of the placid offices of the civil service and into public and political arenas where arguments and debates were livelier and more visceral.

Even before a Social Credit government returned to power in December 1975, efforts were already underway to refocus schools.[38] Newly installed education minister Patrick McGeer, a UBC professor of medicine, advanced the idea of a "core curriculum" drafted but never finalized by the previous government.[39] Henceforth, curriculum materials would be classified into three categories, McGeer declared, "the material which must be learned, that which should be learned, and that which may be learned."[40]

Pursuing the idea of making secondary schooling available to all since the 1950s had shifted the purpose of high schools from "screening to retaining" agencies, to use UBC historian J.D. Wilson's valuable definition.[41] It also changed bureaucratic indicators of success. The intellectually distinguished McGeer easily recognized that, in government circles, retention rates, and number of graduates produced—in other words quantitative measures—were trumping high scholastic standards and the careful selection of the most intellectually able for advancement—in other words, measures of quality. A return to a core curriculum, he argued, was but the first step in a plan to restore provincial control over curriculum that would see the re-introduction of provincially set grade 12 examinations in 1984.[42] In the short run, imposing a core curriculum helped intensify the system's focus on essential subjects. However, it did nothing to quell the swelling torrent of demands for social programs and services that were engulfing the education ministry, schools, and school board offices, as established social structures weakened, and as parental and public notions of entitlement blossomed.

Between 1975 and 1989, when a new school act was finally written, educational government remained preoccupied with three tasks—defining and resourcing a school mandate that seemed out of control, dampening rising school costs, and reforming school practices to improve school-community relations and public confidence in provincial education. To these ends, government launched a handful of "school reform" initiatives, for want of a better term. These initiatives included: McGeer's core curriculum in 1976; minister Brian Smith's 1980 educational fact-finding tour; the introduction of public sector spending restraints in 1983; the 1985 educational survey, *Let's Talk About Schools;* and the 1987 establishment of a royal commission to examine the enlargement of the school mandate and other vexing issues that divided the educational community.[43] Each initiative served in its own way to document the rising state of government and community frustration with public education, as well as the increasing complexity of the public system.

Release of the royal commission's report on August 4, 1988, the largest and most comprehensive study of provincial schools in 30 years, launched an ambitious reform initiative inside educational government. After careful study, the commission had concluded that nothing was fundamentally wrong with public education. Two changes, however, would improve the system. First, the school's social role had become bloated, the commission declared, impairing the system's "ability to discharge its primary educational objectives."[44] "Imposing such responsibilities on schools," the commission continued, "has generally obscured their primary function as institutions for learning and . . . has led to questions about their general educational effectiveness."[45] "The school is not an institution that can stand alone in educating or caring for the young," it concluded.[46] Intellectual development, it ruled, was the school's greatest mission; everything else was secondary.[47] The commission also recommended that new structures be created to give parents and students greater opportunity for educational choice, diversity, and freedom. The report was heralded, potentially, as "the most profound provincial effort at school reform in Canadian education," and warmly received by government, educators, and the public.[48]

Using the commission's report as a platform, government hired a small brigade of educational consultants and began a massive school reform program known as the "Year 2000." Based on notions of continuous learning, an integrated curriculum, non-graded learning situations, and anecdotal report cards, the program sought "to provide children with learning experiences that nurture and sustain the positive self-esteem of all learners."[49] The new program for schools, reformers advised, would be comprised of three levels—primary (kindergarten to grade 3), intermediate (grade 4 to grade 10), and graduation (grades 11 and 12)—through which youngsters would proceed at their own pace, free from the barriers of grade levels and designated amounts of material to be covered annually.

Over a period of three years, it became apparent that Year 2000 reforms were quite different, and considerably more radical, than anything the commission intended. In fact, the consultants that government hired to spearhead the reform effort appeared inclined to overthrow traditional bodies of knowledge and instructional processes. Finally, after nearly four years of programmatic difficulties, including a year-long firestorm of intense parental and public criticism, government's damage control kicked into action. As the new school year began in September 1993, NDP Premier Mike Harcourt stepped to the microphones and said: "To put it bluntly the report card on Year 2000 is in and it's failed the grade."[50]

The system-wide chaos produced by the Year 2000 paled in comparison to the havoc it created inside educational government. It destroyed the education ministry's reputation, decimated the morale of the civil service in charge of schools, and led to the downsizing of the ministry's ranks and scope of operations. Cabinet imposed far tighter controls over the day-to-day affairs of the education ministry by disbanding the deputy's council and removing its authority to make policy decisions.[51] Clumsy implementation of poorly conceived reforms had cost the ministry its two greatest assets—government's confidence in its civil service, and the faith of educators across the province who believed the civil service knew what it was doing.

The Year 2000, in effect, became a self-administered coup de grâce for a government department already in a state of drift and denial. The roots of the ministry's problems could be traced back to 1972, when the education department was still a cohesive and mostly horizontal organization headed by a deputy minister, six superintendents who managed relatively small divisions, and 14 "special officials." With clerical staff and 59 district superintendents assigned to the field, the entire civil service complement, numbering only 136, was responsible for governing and administering 1,515 schools, four universities, and 10 community colleges.[52] Few at this time could dispute the broad reach of the education department's authority, the experience of its officers, or the good sense it generally showed in overseeing the province's educational affairs. It was a "top notch organization," in the words of the deputy minister at the time, marked by "a strong sense of purpose" that pervaded the whole department.[53]

However, as the school's mandate expanded in the 1970s, the education department, now designated a "ministry," ballooned from 136 to 598 staff members by 1979, illustrating that post-colonial administrations everywhere, as a British civil servant drily observed in the 1940s, produced "more government instead of good government."[54] By this time, the ministry's budget had increased five-fold, even though 59 superintendents (formerly inspectors) had abandoned government service for district employment and a score of officials had been re-assigned to a separate post-secondary ministry that would soon swell, itself, in numbers to several hundred people.

Enlarging the school's mandate at the provincial level led to a multiplication of school programs and services in local schools. It also re-bureaucratized school government. Again, by way of perspective, in 1972 the education bureau's functions were confined to six branches—administrative services, field services, instructional services, post-secondary services, special services and technical-vocational services. By 1992, the ministry had mushroomed to 29 different "branches and functions" to oversee new facilities and initiatives in schools, even after the field services unit was closed and post-secondary responsibilities consigned to another ministry.[55]

Incessant personnel changes at political and senior civil service levels in the 1980s and 1990s intensified the ministry's confusion and obscured its vision even more. These changes contrasted sharply with the continuity that historically characterized British Columbia's education office.[56] In the first 81 years of public school history, six senior civil servants presided over educational affairs as provincial superintendents of education and, after 1931, as deputy ministers.[57] Put another way, a total of 12 superintendents or deputies administered the system during the province's first 114 years, each lasting nearly 10 years on average.[58] By the 1980s, however, the deputy's office and the minister's office were becoming organizational carousels where few elected or appointed officials remained for long. In the seven-year period between 1989 and 1996 seven deputies attempted to manage the agenda for educational government. One deputy-a-year hardly constituted a model of stable leadership by any standard, a problem made even worse when experienced and savvy civil servants were replaced with inexperienced people.[59] Things improved after this time, but only barely with deputies' terms averaging slightly over two years.

Nor did education ministers prove much more durable. Between 1980 and 1996, 11 ministers were in charge of the portfolio, averaging about a year and a half each. Some years were worse than others: 1985 witnessed three individuals in the minister's chair; 1996 saw four. By the 1990s, a minister's tenure had shrunk to about a year, too brief a term for any official to accomplish much.[60] Between 1997 and 2005, another seven ministers were handed responsibility for education, again they averaged little more than a year in office. Discontinuity at the top, coupled with major ministry restructurings every two years and episodic downsizings, led naturally to a climate of bureaucratic tentativeness and, occasionally, paralysis.[61]

Small wonder the ministry seemed aimless and in a perpetual quest for its own identity and mission after the mid-1990s, particularly when key managerial positions once held by educators were re-staffed with individuals who knew something about government and administration but virtually nothing about education. Political and public outcries for greater measurement and control of school costs—and for demonstrating greater fiscal responsibility—were now driving the political agenda for schools and were reflected in the recruitment of a new generation of educational bureaucrats who, by the late 1990s, held important positions. Although experienced in other parts of the public service, the new "career bureaucrats" joined the ministry with little pedagogical "know how" or knowledge of the tradecraft necessary to manage educators and get the best out of them. They joined government from backgrounds in finance, law, business administration, and public administration. Most were desk-bound systems specialists who trafficked in statistics and other impersonal forms of authority. Many of the newcomers saw education as just another government portfolio requiring the cost-control discipline of corporate management. Many did not know how to use the data they were gathering to manage the system's operations or pedagogical outcomes.[62]

Government valued their skills because they offered the administrative and financial expertise requisite to streamline a ministry already deemed to be declining in size and importance.[63] The newcomers were generally more comfortable with policy manuals, data processing, financial formulas, and management information systems than with children, teachers, and schools. More to the point, the new recruits owed no cultural or psychological allegiance to public education and flew none of the ideological flags that characterized the ministry's older staff whose careers invariably began as teachers in country classrooms. Such changes in the bureaucracy made it abundantly clear that the days of old-fashioned school officials were over and that a century of professional dominance over public education—in and outside government—was ending. Once the domain of classicists and hard-nosed schoolmen—products themselves of the province's most elite high schools— the long revered education bureau was quietly passing into the hands of accountants as the 1990s ended. Government was becoming a place, to quote the Irish poet Yeats, where "the best lack all conviction." The ministry's relevance to the system continued to decline as government further loosened its grip on curriculum development and school accreditation, moving such decisions increasingly into the hands of textbook publishers and teachers' curriculum committees, respectively.

By the time the 1990s turned into a new millennium, such developments suggested to many educators that, aside from its financial function, the schools ministry was mostly peripheral to local school operations and, therefore, pretty much irrelevant in educational terms. The ministry's "paternal eye," to borrow historian F. Henry Johnson's keen description, no longer seemed focused on the schools.[64] Sadly, this once-great engine of the educational enterprise appeared little more than a shadow of its former self, an organization seemingly dispossessed of its own history and purpose—and lacking any apparent ambition to direct the province's schools.

The ministry's public persona only confirmed this image of indifference. Awash with service plans, risk management strategies, programs to integrate community learning resources, and a host of other initiatives, it appeared more similar to an information clearinghouse than a ministry of government responsible for schools. Small wonder that principals, teachers, and others inside the system saw the ministry as opaque and guarded, isolated from the world of schools it appeared to have abandoned. With few signs of its willingness to provide even rhetorical leadership, or to flex its traditional stewardship role, the ministry reduced itself to two pedestrian functions—measuring aspects of the system's educational performance using criteria not always well understood or appreciated by teachers or parents and serving as a "cash cow" to keep public schooling financially liquid—but only just.

A Rising Tide of Teacher Influence and Power

The third and final factor that changed the character of education in British Columbia was the inexorable growth of teacher influence and power. Nothing influenced the educational world in the decades since 1972—or the relationships between teachers and government—quite as profoundly as two developments that occurred in teachers' ranks between 1961 and 1975, namely the impressive rise in teachers' academic credentials and the BCTF's "conversion to partisanship," as UBC political scientist Marlene Yri termed it.[65] As these events became intertwined, they would change forever the face of public schooling in British Columbia.

Throughout much of public education's first century, scant academic preparation had sullied teachers' reputation and retarded the profession's development and status. During the first half of the twentieth century, it was commonplace for teachers—especially in rural and elementary schools—to enter teaching upon the completion of grade 10 or, sometimes, junior matriculation, followed by a brief stint at normal school that might range anywhere from a mere two months to a year.[66] By permitting "persons of insufficient training to instruct our children, we have endorsed the devaluation of our education as a whole," the BCSTA complained to the Chant commission in the late 1950s.[67]

By the early 1960s, however, the culture of teaching was changing. Increasing numbers of teachers were returning to Victoria College (until 1956 the Provincial Normal School in Victoria) or UBC to upgrade their credentials. By 1972, the education department could proudly boast for the first time that the "percentage of teachers (including part-time teachers) with at least one university degree has gone over 60 per cent," a jump of nearly 57 per cent from the previous year. Credit for the post-1960 rise in teachers' qualifications could largely be attributed to the BCTF and, as UVic's Alastair Glegg has observed, to the provincial government's recruitment drives overseas which brought many highly qualified teachers to the province.[68] After mid-century, the federation had also resolutely encouraged its membership to burnish their educational qualifications through in-service, specialist training, and university study.

Portents of the federation's rising professionalism were manifest in 1961 when three federation representatives were appointed to each of the education department's curriculum committees for elementary and secondary schools. Such developments were watched carefully by personnel inside educational government. By 1966, the department's curriculum chief, the scholarly John Meredith, was lamenting that curriculum control, a responsibility zealously guarded by provincial authorities, was passing out of government's hands and into the hands of others.[69] Expansion of the BCTF's own specialist associations in the 1960s and 1970s further signalled that teachers were consolidating their influence over curricular and instructional domains. It seemed only a matter of time before emerging professional values clashed with those of the bureaucracy. The federation's 1967 annual general meeting extolled a larger role for teachers in setting school policy.[70] "British Columbia had for the first time a provincial teaching force that now appeared ready, if necessary, to do battle over education," Simon Fraser University's (SFU) David Eberwein concluded in his study of collective bargaining.[71]

Apart from straining relations with government, teachers were also making trustees nervous by their increasing involvement in school board elections. At the 1967 BCSTA convention, delegates passed a resolution requesting government to amend the *Public Schools Act* in such a way that would preclude teachers from election as school trustees "if education is to serve society rather than its own establishment."[72] In 1971, the Social Credit government deemed teachers ineligible to run in school board elections but the incoming NDP government overturned this prohibition the following year.

Demonstrating a new zest for professional leadership, the federation convened an in-house educational commission on the future of public education and issued a 1968 report, *Involvement: The Key to Better Schools*, authored by D.B. MacKenzie, W.V. Allester, Mrs. L.A. Haney and R.J. Carter (who would be recruited into government within a decade).[73] The commission's report reflected the heady pedagogical exuberance of the 1960s, and envisioned an era in which public resources for schooling would prove limitless.[74] Among its 189 recommendations, the federation proclaimed the importance of many "big ticket" items: individualized programs for students; continuous progress and a grade-free system; greater decision-making authority for teachers; interdisciplinary study, student self-evaluation and anecdotal report cards; elimination of scholastic aptitude tests, I.Q. tests, corporal punishment, and occupational classes; school-based textbook selection; and full partnership between government and the BCTF in curricular policies and decisions.[75] On the surface, the report revealed a panorama of changes that were dazzling educators elsewhere across the western world at the time.

On a deeper level, however, the report was freighted with something else—a broad statement of intent that outlined the pedagogical territory the BCTF was seeking to contest. *"Involvement,"* Bruneau claims, armed teachers with the "confidence that they could occupy the vacuum" in policy making that was crippling the education department as legislative priorities shifted from grades 1 to 12 to the post-secondary sector.[76] After nearly a half century of waiting in the wings of educational decision making, teachers were now pushing their way onto centre stage with the *Involvement* report, angling for ways to unlock the structures that historically governed how schools were run, what was taught, what was learned, and what was measured. No longer would the BCTF be a "second-order structure," traditionally subservient to the primacy of powerful local teacher associations.[77] By 1968, the federation had arrived as the province's most important educational organization, ensuring that teachers' power was every bit as centralized as the power in educational government. According to Bruneau, 1968 signified "a great divide in the history of B.C. education . . . the start of a chain of events leading to overt political action in a provincial election campaign, and to unprecedented internal politicalization on a wide range of social-educational problems."[78]

Great ambitions were matched by more truculent behaviours on the part of federation leaders. Glimmers of a change away from the old strategies of quiet persuasion and negotiation could be detected as far back as the early 1960s when teachers began to press school boards more openly to extend local bargaining beyond salaries and benefits by including workload and class size considerations. These demands reflected a shift in emphasis, UVic historian James London suggests, from teachers who firmly believed their "prime concern . . . should be the furtherance of public education" to those who "steadfastly considered the main goal of their organization to be the economic welfare of its members."[79] In the optics of the freedom-conscious 1960s, any effort by government to stall discussions about enlarging bargaining conditions was naturally viewed as a "denial of teachers' basic right to collective bargaining." By 1966, such things were leading teachers to talk of a strike.[80]

Teachers' aspirations, however, were transcending the achievement of more than contract provisions. Summing up his year in office, federation president J. Harley Robertson emphasized the membership's changing attitude in 1967: "Teachers have shown that they no longer wish to be cast in a submissive role in education. The growing militancy has led teachers directly to campaign on class size, to act politically, to use publicity in their areas of interest [and] to seek support for their educational demands."[81] By 1969, the federation's new president Tom Hutchinson was warning: "Teacher power is only a beginning," asserting further that the federation had to "become political" and, if necessary "engage in militant action."[82] Teachers were about to cross two lines never crossed before—one leading to partisan political action and one, perhaps even more dangerous, leading teachers to contest an elected government's right to determine public policy in schooling.

Such political proclamations about the manifest destiny of teacher power clearly announced that teachers were no longer willing to be taken for granted in political, educational or, indeed, fiscal matters. Not surprisingly, this new stridency put the federation on a collision course with the education department and, even more so, with the conservative-minded and fiscally prudent Social Credit government.[83]

The rising mood of teacher militancy in the 1960s has been traced to the fact that the federation was a "predominantly young organization" comprised of teachers with "no more than six years' experience."[84] "Many were fresh out of university," journalist Crawford Kilian reported, "at a time when campuses were alive with new ideas that questioned authority" and they quickly became "frustrated and angered" with government's control of educational power.[85] Yri's study of the federation's history from 1966 to 1972 contends that at least five factors coalesced to drive teachers toward partisan politics: the social activism of the 1960s and the rising militancy of teachers elsewhere; the reduction of teachers' bargaining rights by the Social Credit government; a struggle for power between old and new factions inside the federation; the BCTF's growing financial clout and influence; and, finally, the education department's stagnation and the government's shift in provincial priorities to post-secondary education.[86]

Teacher militancy was variously expressed. *B.C. Teacher* editorials roundly criticized the government's building program. The teachers' 1969 "apple" campaign (so named because of the federation's use of an apple logo to separate "teacher friendly" from other legislative candidates) greatly elevated the province's political temperature, as did public attempts by the teachers' federation to challenge funding levels. Bennett's Social Credit government admittedly did little to placate teachers or the federation. Caught up in the province's own remarkable post-war development, the premier and his long-time education minister, Leslie Peterson, could—and did—argue plausibly that money was tight. Skyrocketing inter-provincial migration between 1961 and 1966 had produced annual compound growth rates for British Columbia that exceeded the numbers of newcomers arriving in other regions of great growth, including California, South America, and Asia.[87] Infrastructural costs for "highways, roads, and bridges" to accommodate this migration proved nothing short of staggering.[88]

Educational developments—and the costs that accompanied them—were equally dramatic. Pupil populations in British Columbia schools had swelled from 125,135 in 1944-1945 to 534,523 in 1971-1972, a steep rise of 427 per cent. Teachers' ranks grew even more quickly, climbing from 4,354 to 22,840, an increase of 524 per cent during this period. Pupil participation had also increased in breathtaking fashion "not because of legal requirements, but because of social and parental pressure," that associated schooling with economic and social mobility, as one provincial official explained.[89] Pupil retention rates for grades 1 to 12, in fact, jumped from around 32 per cent in 1932 to somewhere between 85 and 92 per cent by 1970.[90]

Government's alarm over the escalating costs of schooling seemed reasonable under the circumstances. Between 1945 and 1972, total public expenditures on education rose from $13.7 million to nearly $558 million annually, or by more than 4,000 per cent. Over this time, the provincial government's expenditures on education climbed even more impressively, rocketing from slightly more than $5 million annually in 1945 to more than $383 million in 1972, a jump of more than 7,600 per cent.[91]

Looked at another way, when public schooling began in the 1870s the province spent about five per cent of its total expenditures on schools; by the turn of the twentieth century, this had risen to about 12 per cent; by 1951, it had reached 15 per cent; and, by 1971, educational spending constituted about 33 percent of total provincial expenditures. Educational budgets almost doubled in the five-year period from 1966 to 1971.[92] Viewed over a longer perspective: during the 24-year period from 1947 to 1971, school budgets increased 35-fold.[93] Or, stated another way, educational expenditures in 1971 surpassed the entire provincial budget in 1962, only nine years earlier, a fact that chilled both politicians and senior members of educational government.[94]

Provincial statistics, of course, masked the shift in costs from local to provincial governments during the first three-quarters of the twentieth century. To illustrate: in 1924, the province paid 38 per cent of public school costs;[95] by 1945, it paid 27 per cent;[96] by 1971, 41 per cent;[97] and, by 1987, 80 per cent.[98] In other words, a disconnection was steadily taking place between school board demands for educational programs and services and local accountability in paying for such things through property taxes. The financial stage had been amply set for the political and fiscal finger pointing that would generally characterize relations between school boards and government after the mid-1970s.

As the 1970s began, the grave condition of public finances prompted the Economic Council of Canada to forecast that, if education and health care spending continued to rise at about nine per cent annually, they would absorb Canada's entire Gross National Product (GNP) by the century's end.[99] In May 1971, deputy minister Joe Phillipson warned delegates at a meeting of secretary treasurers in Kelowna that British Columbia had been spending nearly one-third of provincial income on education. "How much longer can we afford it," he asked? "Bearing in mind the growing demands on health, welfare, and other government services, how much further can we go?"[100] BCSTA president Peter Powell also realized a pivotal moment in school finance was at hand. Speaking at the trustees' convention that same year, he dampened the mood of delegates by declaring: "the golden age is over. The education system is now faced with having to justify the euphoria of these golden years."[101]

Teachers had, in fact, done well financially since the end of the Great Depression. Between 1941 and 1971, only medical doctors surpassed teachers in terms of salary gains.[102] Thus, the government felt obliged to slow increases in capital and operating costs for school districts and to ignore repeated BCTF requests for substantial increases to the pensions of retired teachers.[103] But government's refusal to address the pension issue only stiffened teachers' resolve and, eventually, provoked a one-day teachers' strike on March 19, 1971, a strike supported by 96 per cent of the voting membership.[104]

Relations between government and the teachers' federation continued to deteriorate as the BCTF refused to heed education minister Leslie Peterson's 1968 warning to "stay out of partisan politics."[105] When education minister Donald Brothers, Peterson's successor, introduced a legislative amendment that excused teachers from automatic membership in the BCTF in 1971, the time for retribution was at hand. At the request of teachers, government had legislated federation membership as compulsory in 1947 and, in return, teachers entered into "a tacit agreement not to strike."[106] In a classic moment of political pontification, Brothers pointed out that it cost taxpayers $25,000 to graduate a teacher, before adding: "It seems incongruous . . . that after having [been] qualified and certified by the department of education, a teacher should be compelled to belong to some other organization before having the right to teach within the Province."[107] Although clearly designed to break the back of the teachers' union by reducing federation numbers, the legislation failed miserably. Fewer than 500 of the province's 22,000 teachers chose to revoke their membership.

But the skirmishing between the province and the BCTF was far from over. The following year, the Bennett government instructed school boards to hold referenda for expenditures more than 6.5 per cent above the previous year's budget, effectively "setting teachers' salaries without negotiation."[108] The teachers responded in kind. Prior to the summer election of 1972, a Teachers' Political-Action Committee (TPAC) was formed to raise funds to oppose the re-election of the Social Credit government, thereby circumventing the legal question about whether the BCTF's general revenues could be used to campaign against a political party. Without newspaper headlines or formal notice, both sides had quietly declared war.

The teachers' federation decisively won the next battle in what would turn out to be a long and bitter encounter. After 20 years in power, a Social Credit government well into its dotage was defeated in the late summer of 1972, despite Bennett's unsettling warning to the electorate that "the socialist hordes were at the gates."[109] Thirty-two of the 35 candidates endorsed by TPAC won seats as Dave Barrett's new NDP administration won 41 out of 57 ridings and began its gaffe-ridden "1,000 day" regime.

Emboldened by claims to a newfound professionalism, the federation began to target a smaller workload in the 1970s as "a battle to be won." After 1946, when Vernon teachers first sought to avoid lunchtime supervision chores, teachers had tried unsuccessfully to bargain working conditions, only to be informed by boards that such things were non-negotiable. By the 1970s, less than one-third of local associations enjoyed any form of duty-free lunch break clauses in their contracts.[110] As teachers' association president in West Vancouver, and later president of the BCTF, Kit Krieger, noted: "a local bargaining survey showed that after salaries, workload was most important to teachers. Key specific items included reduced class size and duty-free lunch hours."[111]

These targets would represent only part of a larger suite of workplace items to be negotiated in the decades ahead, including: "firm class size limits;" "preparation time expressed as hours of instruction;" "full professional autonomy and professional control over educational change;" definition of the "work year and the duration of the school day;" and "professional control over teaching."[112] A few local associations also sought additional payment for teacher involvement in extra-curricular activities. An article in a teachers' newsmagazine advised that achieving a "5.5 hour working day," required eliminating homework assignments, as well as "all coaching and refereeing" duties, school-award programs, "volunteer supervision," committee service, "fund-raising" and "social conscience" activities.[113]

As the federation's militancy intensified in the 1970s, its willingness to confront the provincial government increased. Election of the "radical Marxist" Jim MacFarlan, to use Johnson's description, as federation president between 1973 and 1975 brought a new class-consciousness to the BCTF's executive office.[114] Much like the American social reconstructionists of the 1930s, MacFarlan and his supporters believed schools should be used as instruments of social change and that teachers' influence in school management should be broadened through staff committees.[115] At a 1975 principals' conference, Sparwood Secondary's Harry Peebles emphasized the meaning of the federation's shift from "an educational, professional, and welfare organization . . . [in] the late 1960s to a significantly political organization today."[116] Peebles was particularly alarmed that decision making in schools was being corrupted by "power groups with ideological and parochial interests," and by staff committees whose behaviours were "tyrannical."[117] Far more than conditions of work appeared to be on the table of teachers' ambitions.

MacFarlan was certainly not reluctant to exercise his considerable political muscle. Following the NDP's refusal to provide assurances in the 1974 throne speech that class sizes would be reduced, the Surrey teachers voted in favor of a one-day strike and 1,000 arrived to protest at the legislative buildings in Victoria. This action coerced education minister Dailly to arrange an impromptu meeting between the premier and MacFarlan where, according to MacFarlan, "the premier and I negotiated on a completely ad hoc basis and came up with a proposal that called for the government to reduce the pupil-teacher ratio by 1.5 per year over a three-year period."[118] MacFarlan would eventually call twice for the education minister's resignation—once over class size and once regarding Stanley Knight's 1975 dismissal as the education department's research and development chief—marking the only two occasions in provincial school history when the BCTF actually demanded a minister's removal, and an NDP minister at that.[119]

By 1975, two things were becoming obvious: first, governments on either side of the aisle could be pushed around by the teachers' federation; and, second, the historically serene "schools" portfolio of government was now turbulent. In less than a decade, major public policy decisions about schools had shifted from sedate civil service offices to newspaper headlines and lead stories on regional broadcasts, rupturing a longstanding agreement among legislators in all parties, as well as by trustee and teachers' organizations, that negotiations about educational matters could remain confidential and out of public view, and that schools should be kept "out of politics."[120]

Formation of the Teachers' Viewpoint in 1977, a BCTF splinter group, ushered in a "new kind of progressive caucus" to an already activist-minded organization.[121] Fronted at times by Surrey teacher David Chudnovsky, the Teachers' Viewpoint aspired to achieve the same sort of labour solidarity that RTF advocates solicited back in the 1930s and 1940s. As Chudnovsky argued: "It is essential that there be an organized group of B.C. teachers openly and consciously working to build a union with the right to strike—in other words beginning the task of uniting teachers with other workers."[122] In this new workers' union, Chudnovsky saw no place for principals or others who held "primarily management functions," a sure sign of things to come.[123] This militant spirit quickly infected the emergent BCTF executive. Three of the federation's presidents from 1981 to 1987—Larry Kuehn, Pat Clarke, and Elsie McMurphy—all belonged to the Teachers' Viewpoint, as did other officers supporting the executive.[124]

No single event likely contributed to the federation's *sturm und drang* view of the world, or its vision of the hostile environment around it, than the public sector restraint program introduced in 1982 by W.R. "Bill" Bennett, W.A.C.'s son. A deepening recession, rising unemployment, rampant inflation, shrinking revenues, and a growing taxpayer revolt prompted Bill Bennett's Social Credit government to pass two pieces of legislation—the *Public Service Restraint Act* and the *Education Interim Finance Act*—to control soaring education and other public sector costs. Public school spending had totalled about $900 million in 1976; by 1981, with 32,000 fewer students in the system, the provincial budget for schools had mushroomed to $1.6 billion.[125] Between 1980 and 1981 alone, school budgets had jumped by an average of 19 per cent.[126]

Over the next three years, Bennett's government stabilized educational spending by bringing in annual school budgets of $1.55 billion, $1.57 billion, and

$1.7 billion.[127] Although the public sector restraint program did not cut educational spending, it did dampen its rate of increase and, along the way, downsized the number of teachers by eliminating about 2,000 teachers in resource or non-structured positions, thereby returning educational services to 1976 levels. The BCTF fought loudly against the restraint program, joining a unified labour front known as Operation Solidarity to orchestrate a protest rally of some 50,000 people at Empire Stadium in the summer of 1983, a march of 80,000 people in October at the Social Credit Party convention, and a three-day province-wide teachers' strike in November. The high stakes public protests of 1983 demonstrated that the federation had brought itself to a point of "full maturity" as a political organization and, indeed, as an able adversary for government.[128] *Vancouver Province* columnist, Crawford Kilian, a sharp critic of the public restraint program, argued that restraint drove teachers much deeper into the bosom of the labour movement, something they had resisted since the 1940s:

Having been blooded in the province-wide strike, teachers could calmly contemplate the pros and cons of striking locally. In that respect, the teaching profession in B.C. had become permanently more politicized, as it moved closer to the centre of the labour movement. Teachers had begun to see themselves less as aspiring professionals and more as workers, no longer kidding themselves that a university degree and a teaching certificate somehow elevated them above the ranks of the working class. If that was a development deplored by many British Columbians, they had only themselves to blame . . .[129]

Events of 1983, according to former federation president, Ken Novakowski (1989-1992), were "a transformative experience for teachers," a "political act—a protest action, taken as part of a broader labour strategy."[130] In 1985, Kilian portrayed the great conflict between government and the teachers as the "school wars," a description accurate insofar as it conveyed the bitterness and intensity of the struggle. Looking backward, however, it is evident that the province's era of "school wars" has occupied a far greater period than the three years between 1982 and 1985 chronicled in Kilian's book on public sector restraint.[131] The extent of hostilities, in fact, covers a period appreciably longer—some 40 years and still counting since the conflict first began. Over this time, the federation has functioned more often as government's official opposition than the political party actually out of office—especially in matters concerning school policy and public sector spending.

Doubling the size of the BCTF's membership between the 1970s and the 1990s greatly added to the federation's wealth and status, making it the province's largest and most influential educational organization, easily dwarfing the education ministry in importance. Twice, at least, by its own count, the BCTF was instrumental in bringing governments down—notably in 1972 and 1991.[132] Over this time, no union, public sector or otherwise—not even the redoubtable mother-ship of west coast unionism, the B.C. Federation of Labour (BCFL)—has proved a more capable or dangerous adversary for government. Reasons for this reside in various factors, including the BCTF's shrewd political expertise, its virtually inexhaustible resources, education's foundational importance in contemporary society, and the public's historical and sentimental proclivity to take the teachers' side, even when critical of the public system's overall performance.

Certainly, the federation has appeared deft in managing some aspects of its public persona. A notable BCTF triumph in the decades-long struggle for hearts and minds has resided in its success in persuading parents and the public that certain educational outcomes—notably higher thinking, creativity, and love of learning—defy measurement by standardized tests. Such tests, the federation has claimed, do not assess citizenship qualities, social awareness, sound judgment, and other meaningful results that schools produce in young people. And, even when the education ministry developed solid objective measures of district, school, and pupil performance in the early 1980s, circumstances bedeviled government and prevented it from making the results public.[133] Bureaucrats and their political masters were understandably reluctant to circulate management information and student performance data that indicated wide variance in district-to-district and within-district outcomes, lest parents and the public made the absence of system-wide equity and insufficient accountability even more vexing political issues for government to address.

And so, save for school rankings known disdainfully as "league tables," published annually by the conservative-minded Fraser Institute in Vancouver, information about the system's true condition has remained largely out of public view, read mostly by bureaucrats and their political masters inside provincial and local board offices. Despite scant evidence, British Columbians since the time of the *Involvement* report in 1968 have come to accept that "input measures" such as higher teachers' salaries, smaller class sizes, and other improvements in learning conditions somehow constitute more credible measures of educational quality than output results from mathematics and language tests.

Wrong-headed though they may be, such beliefs ensure that the BCTF always holds better pedagogical cards than government, or its agencies, in educational and public policy debates. More than three decades of consistent messaging by the federation about the ills of testing and spending cuts has proved once again that Napoleon was right, "God favours the side with the best artillery."

As a new millennium began, no reading of the provincial tea leaves was required to predict that the BCTF and the British Columbia Liberal Party would quickly find themselves at odds. Even before the 2001 election, when Gordon Campbell's free-enterprise Liberal government won 77 of 79 ridings in the largest electoral landslide in provincial history, the principal part of the script about government-teacher conflict had already been written. The Liberals had stumped on austerity and making education an "essential service." The federation, in response, had paid for a campaign of negative advertising to discredit them. If such things were not sufficient in themselves to destroy relations, a tradition of unresolved contract negotiations inherited from NDP governments in the 1990s remained a festering problem.

In 1993 the *Public Sector Employers Act* was passed, creating six multi-employer associations including one in the K-12 public education sector assigned to coordinate human resource practices, particularly labour relations. The *Act* contemplated a co-governed model whereby each association would balance the interests of employers with the public policy responsibilities of government to the extent that public policy had employment implications.

In 1994 a provincial bargaining model was created with the passage of the *Public Education Labour Relations Act*. The BCPSEA was formed as the accredited agency to bargain on behalf of all districts. Local teacher certifications were dissolved and the BCTF was designated as the bargaining agent for all public school teachers. The move to provincial bargaining did not enjoy BCTF support. Implementation of the new bargaining model was further complicated by the absence of transition provisions that would reconcile the existence of 75 employers, 75 teacher locals, and 75 collective agreements within an overarching provincial framework. Presence of new bargaining authorities and structure, however, failed to resolve vexing issues. Year after year, the employers' association and the BCTF continued to disagree about contract provisions, obliging government to become involved in bargaining in 1996 and to legislate a contract in 1998.

A historically divisive management-labour climate grew even more rancorous after 2001 when government embarked on a series of initiatives including the codification of rights for parents and amending the *Labour*

Relations Code to designate K-12 public education an "essential service," as Social Credit governments had earlier designated. Government also continued limitations on public sector compensation that had been enacted in various forms since the early 1990s. Two pieces of legislation introduced at the end of January 2001 would prove particularly controversial—Bill 27, the *Education Services Collective Agreement Act* and Bill 28, the *Public Education Flexibility and Choice Act*.

The *Education Services Collective Agreement Act* was for the most part back-to-work legislation that provided terms for a return to work. The *Act* also provided the basis for structural change that would affect some districts and, potentially, the sector as a whole. Specifically, the bill required that consolidation of local teacher agreements be completed for those districts amalgamated in December 1996 that still had not consolidated their agreements. Finally, the *Act* provided for a review of the teacher-public school employer bargaining structure.

Bill 28, the *Public Education Flexibility and Choice Act*, fulfilled the government's commitment to place school organization issues within a legislative framework, removing them from collective bargaining, collective agreements, and the rule-making process that characterizes labour relations between unions and employers. Narrowing the scope of teacher-employer collective bargaining, the stated intention of the *School Act* amendments in Bill 28, aimed to provide a new framework for instructional planning in schools—one that involved parents, teachers, principals, school boards, and newly created school planning councils. Bill 28 also sought to take into account that class size, class composition, and the organization of schools, were complicated public policy matters that were shaped by the interplay of economic, social, and human resource factors. In effect, the *Act* moved school organization matters away from the collective agreement and collective bargaining process and placed them in the realm of law and public policy.

Two broad schools of thought surrounded the question about whether school organizational matters should be legislatively determined, or whether they should constitute items for bargaining. The government's position, with general support from the British Columbia Principals' and Vice-Principals' Association (BCPVPA), the British Columbia Council of Parent Advisory Councils (BCCPAC), as well as some trustees and parents, was that school organizational issues are matters of general public importance to many others in the educational and provincial community apart from teachers—including parents, principals, school boards, and the public at large—and, therefore, they should be addressed as public policy matters, not as bargaining chips in a collective agreement.[134]

The BCTF strongly opposed this view and, in May 2002, filed a petition in the British Columbia Supreme Court alleging that passage of Bills 27 and 28 violated teachers' constitutional rights. The case was held over pending an action by health unions against Bill 29, the *Health and Social Services Delivery Implementation Act*. The Health Services case found its way to the Supreme Court of Canada in 2007 with the court eventually finding that collective bargaining enjoyed a measure of protection under the *Canadian Charter of Rights and Freedoms* and that government had erred in failing to consult with the unions before introducing new legislation.[135]

The BCTF case was not heard in the British Columbia Supreme Court until November 2010. The BCTF took the position before Madam Justice S. Griffin that changes to the *School Act* in 2002 were unconstitutional because they prohibited collective bargaining on matters related to class size, class composition, non-enrolling staffing ratios, and hours of work (referred to as "working conditions provisions") and, also, removed offending collective agreement provisions from the collective agreement. Along with challenging the legislation, the BCTF also alleged that government and the BCPSEA, the employer's bargaining agent, offended the protection for collective bargaining provided by the *Charter* by engaging in bad faith bargaining in 2001. Finally, the BCTF claimed that the 2002 *Amendment Act* that merged collective agreements in amalgamated school districts was similarly unconstitutional.[136]

The province's objectives in passing the 2002 legislation, the British Columbia Attorney General argued in response, were "to provide greater flexibility to school boards to manage class size and composition issues, to respond to choices of parents and students, and to make their own decisions on better use of facilities and human resources," as Justice Griffin would later summarize them.[137] The Court's decision was released in April 2011 and adopted the precedent set by the Supreme Court of Canada in the Health Services case by ruling that the Freedom of Association protected by the *Charter* included the right to the "process" of collective bargaining. Justice Griffin decided that the government's 2002 legislation interfered with this process and that the interference was substantial.

However, the Court also noted that, when the legislation was introduced in 2002, "the state of the law in Canada was such that the government likely did not anticipate that collective bargaining was protected by s. 2 (d) of the *Charter*."[138] On the matter of "working conditions provisions," the Court found that the process used by government negated any process for voluntary good faith bargaining and consultation, whereas the process used in relation to the *Amendment Act* left open a process for future good faith negotiation. The Court rejected the argument that the BCPSEA failed to bargain in good faith in 2001 and 2002. Although the BCPSEA sought policy direction from government to inform its bargaining approach, there was simply no evidence to suggest government acted in league with the BCPSEA to negotiate, or otherwise act in bad faith, prior to the passage of legislation.

Altogether, the Court found that only the "working conditions provisions" breached the *Charter* guarantee of Freedom of Association. And, although the Court declared them to be invalid, the declaration of invalidity was suspended for a year to afford government time to address the decision's implications. Whether government will revisit pre-2002 legislative provisions, or enact new legislation to address the deficiencies that prompted the Court's decision, remains to be seen.

Bills 27 and 28 also prompted other developments that set the stage for the 2004-2005 round of bargaining. Infuriated with what amounted to a salary freeze and the government's disinterest in continuing to reduce class sizes, nearly 90 per cent of teachers voted on September 27, 2005 to engage in job action, threatening more severe measures if negotiations failed. Anxious to avoid direct confrontation, the provincial government passed legislation extending the teachers' 2004-2005 contract to June 2006. Following this, the BCPSEA successfully petitioned the British Columbia Labour Relations Board (BCLRB) to declare any form of strike action illegal, arguing that as a consequence of the legislative extension an agreement was in force and job action was not permitted.

Enraged by government's high-handedness and the BCPSEA's success with the labour relations board, the teachers' federation called a strike on October 7, 2005 leaving 600,000 students and their parents stranded for the best part of two weeks. Some 25,000 support staff workers, predominantly represented by the Canadian Union of Public Employees (CUPE) workers also walked off the job.[139] "Thousands of public school teachers across British Columbia are out on strike," national columnist Andrew Coyne observed, adding caustically, "What else is new?"[140] In support of teachers, the BCFL engineered a "Day of Protest" that involved 20,000 people and shut down public services in Victoria while protestors occupied the legislative lawns. The BCPSEA quickly filed a complaint with the British Columbia Supreme Court and the court ruled the BCTF acted in contempt and ordered the teachers to return to work.

In the best traditions of provincial politics, the events that followed were pure political theatre—something never out of season in British Columbia. Good struggled against evil and heroes wrestled with villains. Liberal premier, Gordon Campbell, championed good government, the court's ruling, and children's right to attend school. Federation president, Jinny Sims, cast herself and the union as public education's staunchest defenders, holding aloft the banner for smaller classes and greater school spending. Sims and the BCTF justified their defiance of the law by claiming education was not an essential service and that teachers' bargaining rights had been unfairly constrained by an imposed contract.[141] Heightening the drama, Sims portrayed the BCTF's response as an act of civil disobedience and likened herself to American civil rights heroine, Rosa Parks, although Sims blundered badly by referring to the activist as "Nora Parks."

During the strike's early days, Sims and the teachers outflanked government on the public relations front, easily winning the battle for public approval. But, as the strike stretched into the second week, public patience and parental sympathy for teachers wore thin. Parents grumbled that teachers had "made their point" and it was time to return to school. The press agreed. "This madness has to end," a *Vancouver Sun* editorial remarked in frustration: "The government must start talking to teachers . . . They are continents apart, hostile and suspicious of each other's motives."[142] This, of course, was not new "news" to anyone west of the Rockies since the 1960s.

Government acted immediately to bring closure by appointing Vince Ready, a skilled labour mediator, who quickly brought matters to a head by forcing both sides to a settlement. Sensing a slide in public support—and realizing little more could be achieved—Sims recommended the settlement to teachers with "great reluctance."[143] This agreement set the stage for the next round of bargaining, this time under a bargaining model proposed by mediator Ready. In the late hours of June 30, 2006, the BCPSEA and the BCTF agreed to a 16 per cent increase spread over five years plus a signing bonus available to all public sector workers who were able to conclude agreements before the expiry of their agreements. Ready, also tasked with recommending a bargaining structure, released his final report in February 2007. He suggested the structure that yielded the only negotiated collective agreement in 2006 should be adopted as the basis for bargaining. Government and the BCPSEA accepted Ready's recommendation. The BCTF did not.

In retrospect, the 2005 strike should be seen for exactly what it was—simply another unhappy chapter in a lengthy history of unsettled labour relations in British Columbia schools. Strike action began the story in 1971. After three bitter years of public sector warfare from 1982 to 1985 a royal commission was convened in 1987, in large part to arrange an educational truce in a conflict that could already be traced back almost two decades. A two-year study of the province's educational problems by the commission, the establishment of new decision-making and communications structures, the infusion of vast amounts of public money for system renewal by two governments, and the fact that government and the teachers had virtually punched themselves to a standstill, produced little more than a brief interlude in the fighting.

Sadly, nothing was solved, nothing was learned save, perhaps, for this: if insanity can be defined as expecting the repetition of certain behaviours to produce different outcomes, the organizations most responsible for controlling the public system continue to reside close to the edge of madness. Simply put, save for brief episodes of short-lived tranquility, governments of all political stripes—Social Credit, NDP, and Liberal—have found themselves in a state of almost perpetual conflict with the BCTF for 40 years. Even the issues don't markedly change—salaries, conditions of work, compulsory membership in the teachers' union, class size and composition, and the right to strike continue to remain hot-button issues.

Notes

1. ARPS, 1971-1972.

2. Ibid., D-15 and British Columbia Department of Education, *One Hundred Years*, 74.

3. Maxwell A. Cameron, *Report of the Commission of Inquiry into Educational Finance* (Victoria: King's Printer, 1945).

4. Johnson, *A History of Public Education in British Columbia*, 125.

5. This figure is approximate. See British Columbia Department of Education, *One Hundred Years*, 68.

6. The idea of restructuring small school districts into larger governance units goes back to C.C. McKenzie's tenure as provincial superintendent when he amalgamated several districts in Saanich. Cameron's post-war plan, however, owed its existence more directly to the consolidation exercise undertaken in the Peace River region during the 1930s when school inspector, Bill Plenderleith, collapsed 63 isolated districts into one large region for administrative purposes.

7. Johnson, *A Brief History of Canadian Education*, 110-111.

8. Cameron, *Report of the Commission of Inquiry*, 36.

9. The notion that district consolidation, and the emergence of larger local systems, would solve a multitude of issues without some unforeseen consequences was arguably naïve.

10. Two general trends of the post-1945 era—the rising costs of schooling and the gradual transfer in responsibility for school support from local to provincial authorities—have had important implications for school governance and are noted in: John C. Chalmers, *Schools of the Foothills Province: The Story of Public Education in Alberta* (Toronto: University of Toronto Press, 1967), 334. In British Columbia, the provincial government provided approximately 80 per cent of school revenues in 1987, compared to about 38 per cent in 1924. See: British Columbia Royal Commission on Education, *A Legacy for Learners* (Victoria: Queen's Printer, 1988), 153; and Johnson, *A History of Public Education in British Columbia*, 97.

11. In separate conversations, two northern veteran superintendents, Terry McBurney and Alan Newberry, referred to the Stikine district (School District No. 87) as "larger than France."

12. London, *Public Education Public Pride*, 225.

13. Debate about this issue could be traced back to 1911 when Vancouver superintendent, W.P. Argue, resigned in protest following provincial school tsar Alexander Robinson's decision to refuse the Vancouver School Board the right to appoint a local school chief. See Fleming, "In the Imperial Age and After," 168-169.

14. British Columbia School Trustees Association, "Brief to the Royal Commission on Education," 1959; British Columbia Teachers' Federation, "Brief to the Royal Commission on Education," 1959; in S.N.F. Chant, J.E. Liersch, and R.P. Walrod, *Report of the Royal Commission on Education* (Victoria: Queen's Printer, 1960), 28 and 31.

15. British Columbia School Trustees Association, "Brief to the Royal Commission on Education," 31.

16. Alexander Robinson's correspondence with J.J. Ross, Edmonton, Alberta, 23 October 1919, Superintendent of Education's Letterbooks, PABC, Vol. 189, 9280.

17. Chant, *Report of the Royal Commission on Education*, 68-69. The stumbling block was the civil service classification scale, or "salary tree," as it was more commonly known, where increments among "grades" were small and so tightly prescribed that even long serving and powerful deputy ministers like S.J. Willis (1919-1946) could not influence the civil service commission to secure relief for his senior staff.

18. In the "political battlefield" that was public education after the late 1960s, it was difficult, London admits, for the BCSTA "to maintain a neutral position" between government and the teachers. See London, *Public Education Public Pride*, 273.

19. Interview with Jack Fleming, Saanich, British Columbia, 15 June 1995.

20. This point was made emphatically in Thomas Fleming, "From Educational Government to the Government of Education: The Decline and Fall of the British Columbia Ministry of Education, 1972-1996," *Historical Studies in Education*, Vol. 15, No. 2 (Fall 2003): 210-236.

21. Fleming, "In the Imperial Age and After," 161.

22. Fleming, *The Principal's Office and Beyond, Volume 1*, 139-150 and 155-167, describes the effects of bureaucratizing city schools on principals, school staff, and children.

23. For a chronicle of this collapse, see Fleming, "From Educational Government to the Government of Education: The Decline and Fall of the British Columbia Ministry of Education."

24. In contrast to the "schools" side of the department that languished without new ideas, the "colleges and universities" side prospered greatly throughout the 1960s. Creation of two new universities in 1962—the University of Victoria and Simon Fraser University, together with a blueprint for a community college system— signalled that government's energies would increasingly be directed toward meeting public demands for access to higher learning, and away from its historical focus on expanding the public school system. By 1965, first-year enrollments at the province's three universities were exceeding the number of students that had graduated from the "university program," in high schools the year before, reflecting the new importance assigned to higher education.

25. British Columbia Department of Education, *One Hundred Years*, 68.

26. Statistics Canada, "Operating and capital expenditures of public school boards on elementary and secondary education, Canada and provinces, selected years, 1900 to 1974, Table W275-300" and "Expenditures on elementary and secondary education, by source of funds, Canada, selected years, 1950 to 1974, Table W301-306." http://www.statcan.gc.ca/pub/11-516-x/sectionw/4147445-eng.htm, retrieved 19 March, 2008.

27. Ibid.

28. Stan Persky, *Son of Socred* (Vancouver: North Star Books, 1979), 138. I am grateful to my colleague Helen Raptis at the University of Victoria for pointing out that the education minister in 1970-1971 assumed responsibility for approving curriculum whereas, previously, the deputy minister had enjoyed this authority.

29. Ibid.

30. In the eight-year period between 1975 and 1983, women's participation in the national labour force rose by 15 per cent for women aged 25 to 44, and about 12 per cent for women between 45 and 54 years. By 1983, almost 52 per cent of married women with pre-school children worked—a significant increase over the 34 per cent who did so in 1975. In the same period, married women with children aged six to 15 increased their labour force participation from 47 per cent to nearly 70 per cent. See British Columbia Royal Commission on Education, *A Legacy for Learners*, 31.

31. Fleming, "Our Boys in the Field," 300. For another discussion of external pressures on the British Columbia education ministry regarding the schooling of minorities, see: Helen Raptis, "Dealing with Diversity: Multicultural Education in British Columbia, 1872-1981," Unpublished Ph.D. dissertation, University of Victoria, 2001.

32. Hansard, 1976 Legislative Session: 1st Session, 31st Parliament, Monday 12 April 1976, 873.

33. Ibid.

34. One of the first government documents to propose a more coherent way of managing school costs was "Financial Management of Education in British Columbia," a background paper written by Barry Anderson in January 1984.

35. E.M. Carlin, "Excerpts of Interviews with Deputy Ministers of Education, 1970-1984," Unpublished report, University of British Columbia, 1984, 19, 21-23, and 29-30.

36. Robert Dennison, "A Study of the Prince George Citizen, 1957-1961: Editorial Reaction to Education and the Chant Commission on Education (1960)," Unpublished major paper in Social and Educational Studies, University of British Columbia, 1984.

37. Thomas Fleming, "Accountability: Some Considerations of a Continuing Educational Dilemma," *The Journal of Educational Thought*, Vol. 12, No. 1 (April 1978), 28-36.

38. Ibid. The core curriculum had been originally conceived as the heart of a curriculum that would "allow students to comprehend and master the total curriculum."

39. Ibid.

40. Hansard, 1977 Legislative Session: 2nd Session, 31st Parliament, Thursday 13 January 1977, 4.

41. J.D. Wilson, "The Evolving School: A Canadian Historical Perspective," in Evelina Orteza y Miranda and Romulo F. Magsino (Eds.), *Teaching, Schools and Society* (Basingstoke: Falmer Press, 1990), 22.

42. Such exams were set "to ensure that grade 12 students meet consistent provincial standards of achievement" and to treat all students "equitably when applying for admission to post-secondary institutions."

43. British Columbia Provincial School Review Committee, *Let's Talk About Schools: A Report to the Minister of Education and the People of British Columbia* (Victoria: Ministry of Education, 1985).

44. British Columbia Royal Commission on Education, *A Legacy for Learners*, 72.

45. Ibid., 8.

46. Ibid.

47. As far as the contents of learning were concerned, the commission suggested focusing the curriculum from grades 1 to 10 around four essential categories of knowledge—the humanities, science, fine arts, and practical arts—and by emphasizing inter-relationships among subjects wherever possible. The program of study for grades 11 and 12 was radically reconceived for youngsters not intending to go on to colleges and universities. It allowed trades and business apprenticeships in and outside schools to qualify for public support, and educational credit for the majority of students who wanted to complete high school without completing senior matriculation.

48. Paul Goldman, "Jump-Starting Educational Reform: Implementing British Columbia's Comprehensive School Act," A paper presented at the Annual Meeting of the University Council for Educational Administration, Pittsburg, PA, 26-28 October 1990, 4. http://eric.ed.gov:80/PDFS/ED325939.pdf, retrieved 2 November 2009.

49. Vaughn Palmer, "A primer on the premier and the edu-crats," *Vancouver Sun*, 23 November 1993, A14.

50. *Times-Colonist*, "Chalk up another NDP fiasco," Thursday, 9 September 1993, A4.

51. Interview with Sam Lim, Victoria, 27 November 1993.

52. ARPS 1972-1973, D15-D87.

53. Joe Phillipson, ""After Dinner Address to the B.C.S.D. Secretary Treasurers' Association," Kelowna, 11 May 1971, 3.

54. British Columbia Department of Education, "Estimates of Expenditures for the Fiscal Year Ending March 1971." See also British Columbia Ministry of Education, Science, and Technology, "Estimates of Expenditure, 1979/80."

55. Among the ministry's new offices were an aboriginal education branch: a business immigration branch; an immigration policy branch; an independent schools branch; an information services branch; a languages and multicultural programs branch; a gender equity and women's programs unit; and a planning and corporate research branch. But even as these new divisions were evolving, deputy ministers and other senior officials were finding it impossible to create the command and control structures necessary to coordinate initiatives among the ministry's many sub-units or, for that matter, to understand what different parts of the organization were actually doing and how they could be linked more effectively. See ARPS 1991-1992, 113-115.

56. Patrick Dunae has pointed out that the 1950s and 1960s appear to be the decades of greatest stability and continuity at the highest levels of educational government with Leslie Peterson serving as minister (1956-1968), J.F.K. English as deputy minister (1958-1965), and E.E. Hyndman as chief inspector of schools (1958-1964). See British Columbia Department of Education, *One Hundred Years*, 91-100.

57. Ibid., 96-97. The provincial superintendent's position was merged with that of the deputy minister in 1931.

58. Ibid.

59. Veteran bureaucrats R.J. "Jim" Carter and Sandy Peel, for example, were followed by the less experienced Valerie Mitchell, Cynthia Morton, Paul Pallan (acting), and Gary Wouters.

60. British Columbia education ministers in the 1980s and 1990s included: Brian Smith (1979-1982), William Vander Zalm (1982-1983), Jack Heinrich (1983-1985), James Hewitt (1985-1985), Tony Brummett (1985-1990), Stan Hagen (1990-1991), Anita Hagen (1991-1993), Art Charbonneau (1993-1996), Paul Ramsey (1996-1996), Moe Sihota (1996-1996), Joy MacPhail (1996-1997), Paul Ramsey (1997-1999), and Gordon Wilson (1999-2000).

61. Growth in ministry ranks rose and fell according to government initiatives and the province's economic state. During the 1980s restraint program, for example, the ministry's size declined from 780 to 435 staff.

62. Evidence of this shift in expertise could be detected as far back as the early 1980s. For a more complete discussion of this change see Fleming, "In the Imperial Age and After," 161-188 and Fleming, "From Educational Government to the Government of Education," 210-236.

63. A staff of some 700 members in the mid-1980s was reduced to about 150 by the mid-1990s. Interview with R.J. Carter, Vancouver, 28 May 1998.

64. Johnson, *A History of Public Education in British Columbia*, 238.

65. Marlene Yri, "The British Columbia Teachers' Federation and Its Conversion to Partisanship, 1966-972," Unpublished M.A. thesis in Political Science, University of British Columbia, 1979.

66. Working teachers could improve their certification either through six-week courses offered at the normal schools by the education department's "summer school of education" or, through education courses at University of British Columbia after 1920.

67. London, *Public Education Public Pride*, 213.

68. ARPS 1971-1972, D15. Alastair Glegg has observed that many highly educated teachers were arriving from the United Kingdom in the late 1950s and early 1960s as a result of vigorous recruiting initiatives by the provincial government. These incoming teachers no doubt helped elevate the percentage of provincial teachers with university degrees.

69. ARPS 1965-1966, F50.

70. David Eberwein, "Teacher Collective Bargaining in B.C. Perspectives on the Vancouver School District," Unpublished M.Ed. thesis, Simon Fraser University, 1995, 22.

71. Ibid.

72. London, *Public Education Public Pride*, 275.

73. British Columbia Teachers' Federation, *The Report of the Commission on Education of the British Columbia Teachers' Federation: Involvement—The Key to Better Schools* (Vancouver: British Columbia Teachers' Federation, 1968.) Mackenzie was a retired assistant superintendent from Vancouver; Allester was the BCTF's director of professional development; Haney was an intermediate supervisor in Burnaby; and Carter was vice-principal at Point Grey Secondary.

74. Many of the BCTF's positions on educational matters in the 1960s were summarized in *Involvement: The Key to Better Schools*.

75. Ibid., 16, 17, 27, 39, 48, 51, 53, 61, 71 and 72.

76. Bruneau, "Still Pleased to Teach," 71.

77. Ibid., 22.

78. Ibid., 64.

79. London, *Public Education Public Pride*, 273.

80. Eberwein, "Teacher Collective Bargaining," 22.

81. Johnson, "V. Revolt: The RTA in British Columbia," 259.

82. Charles S. Ungerleider, "Globalization, Professionalization, and Educational Politics in British Columbia," *Canadian Journal of Educational Administration and Policy*, No. 9 (15 December 1996), 2.

83. Teacher demands for a decisive role in local governance sent a shudder through 1967 BCSTA Convention, prompting delegates to pass a resolution requesting government to amend Section 59 (1) of the *Public Schools Act* to deny teachers' eligibility to serve as trustees, thereby preventing a "significant conflict of interests" (London, *Public Education Public Pride*, 275). A year later W.A.C. Bennett's Social Credit government finally acceded to the trustees' request but, a year later in 1971, the incoming NDP government tore up the amendment and restored the right of teachers to serve on boards (Ibid.). Up to 1968, teachers could run for election on any school board, except the ones employing them. As public representatives, trustees were naturally alarmed at the idea of teachers directly influencing board decisions, or what would later be known as "provider capture." For a broader discussion of this concept, see: Edward B. Fiske and Helen F. Ladd, *When Schools Compete: A Cautionary Tale* (Washington: Brookings Institution Press, 2000), 42.

84. Crawford Kilian, *School Wars: The Assault on B.C. Education* (Vancouver: New Star Books, 1985), 37.

85. Ibid.

86. Yri, "The British Columbia Teachers' Federation and Its Conversion to Partisanship."

87. Fleming and Conway, "Setting Standards in the West," 146.

88. London, *Public Education Public Pride*, 253.

89. C.B. Conway, *Pressure Points and Growing Pains in Beautiful B.C.: Informal Paper* (Toronto: Ontario Institute for Studies in Education, 1971), 7.

90. Ibid., 8. This was calculated as the percentage of "the average elementary-school cohort stream (successive grades 2 to 6)" entering grade 12.

91. ARPS 1971-1972, D 190-191.

92. British Columbia Department of Education, *One Hundred Years*, 90.

93. Ibid.

94. Ibid.

95. Johnson, *A History of Public Education in British Columbia*, 97.

96. ARPS 1971-1972, D-190.

97. Ibid.

98. British Columbia Royal Commission on Education, *A Legacy for Learners*, 153.

99. British Columbia Department of Education, *One Hundred Years*, 15.

100. Phillipson, "After Dinner Address," 7.

101. Cited in London, *Public Education Public Pride*, 262.

102. Bruneau, "Still Pleased to Teach," 43.

103. London, *Public Education Public Pride*, 256.

104. Ibid., 275.

105. Bruneau, "Still Pleased to Teach," 78.

106. Ibid., 42.

107. 1971 Legislative Session: 2nd Session, 29th Parliament, *Hansard*, 2.

108. Bruneau, "Still Pleased to Teach," 79.

109. CBC News, "The 'socialist hordes' break through," http://archives.cbc.ca/politics/provincial_territorial_politics/topics/1637-11304/ retrieved 19 December 2009.

110. *Teacher Newsmagazine*, (April/May 1988), 3. The 21 local associations which achieved some form of duty-free lunch hour agreements with their boards were Fernie, Windermere, Castlegar, Arrow Lakes, Trail, Golden, North Thompson, Langley, Delta, Vancouver, New Westminster, Maple Ridge, Howe Sound, Peace River North, Qualicum, Courtenay, Campbell River, Mission, Vancouver Island North, Creston-Kaslo and Stikine.

111. Ibid.

112. *Teacher Newsmagazine*, Vol. 2, No. 6 (Feb./March 1990), 4.

113. *Teacher Newsmagazine*, Vol. 3, No. 7 (June 1991), 2.

114. Johnson, "V. Revolt: The RTA in British Columbia," 260.

115. These views had been espoused in the 1930s by academics such as John Dewey and his colleagues at Columbia, notably William H. Kilpatrick, John L. Childs, and Bruce Raup. See, for example, William H. Kilpatrick (Ed.), *The Educational Frontier: The Twenty-First Yearbook of the National Society of College Teachers of Education* (Chicago: University of Chicago Press, 1933).

116. Harry M. Peebles, "Administrators in Command," *Proceedings of the Seventh Annual Principals' Conference, 15-18 October, 1975 Fairmont Hot Springs, B.C.*, 48.

117. Ibid., 52.

118. London, *Public Education Public Pride*, 296.

119. Ibid., London reports one of these calls for Mrs. Dailly's resignation.

120. A handful of former school inspectors and district superintendents, as well as senior government officials, made this point emphatically in interviews. They indicated that, prior to the end of the 1960s, a "gentlemen's agreement" existed among politicians in the provincial legislature that "schools should be kept out of politics." Moreover, they claimed that the tilt of educational government for much of the twentieth century was small "l" liberal and, as civil servants, they were generally free to conduct the province's educational business without political interference. These comments were made in various ways by Harold Campbell, John Meredith, Stewart Graham, Les Canty, Joe Phillipson, and Bill Plenderleith, among others. In *Public Education Public Pride* (275), London describes how trustees' president, Peter Powell, sought to create a level of "mutual confidentiality" with the education department and "not . . . to do battle . . . in the news media."

121. Seija Tyllinen, "The History of the Separation of Principals, from the British Columbia Teachers' Federation," Unpublished M.A. Thesis University of British Columbia, 1988, 41.

122. Ibid.

123. Ibid., 42.

124. Ibid., 69 and 85. Tyllinen claims McMurphy renounced her membership in the Teachers' Viewpoint group a few months before her third re-election as president in 1988-1989 in order to form an opposing group called "Teachers for a United Federation."

125. Thomas Fleming, "Restraint, Reform and Reallocation: A Brief Analysis of Government Policies on Public Schooling in British Columbia, 1981-1984," *Education Canada*, Vol. 25, No. 1 (Spring 1985), 6-7.

126. Ibid.

127. Ibid. 9.

128. Tyllinen, "The History of the Separation of Principals," 28.

129. Kilian, *School Wars*, 97.

130. Ken Novakowski, "The Solidarity Strike of 1983," *Teacher Newsmagazine*, Vol. 12, No. 4 (Jan./Feb. 2000), 1.

131. Kilian, *School Wars*.

132. Ken Novakowski, "It's Who We Are," *Teacher Newsmagazine*, Vol. 17, No. 1 (September 2004), 1.

133. These measures were known as "Indicators of Management Performance."

134. During the second reading of Bill 28 on January 26, 2002, Minister of Skills Development and Labour, Graham Bruce, used the term "bargaining chip," in reference to the claim that class sizes were too important to students to be left as a bargaining chip between the BCTF and employers.

135. British Columbia Teachers' Federation v. British Columbia, 2011 BCSC 469, [348] and [375], 88 and 95.

136. British Columbia Teachers' Federation v. British Columbia, 2011 BCSC 469. In addition to challenging the legislation, the BCTF charged that government and, by extension, the BCPSEA engaged in additional unconstitutional conduct by engaging in bad faith bargaining in 2001, leading-up to the passage of Bills 27 and 28. The British Columbia Supreme Court rejected this argument in April 2011, noting that while BCPSEA sought policy direction from government in order to inform its approach to bargaining, there was simply no evidence that the government acted in concert with BCPSEA to negotiate or otherwise act in bad faith in the months leading up to the legislation.

137. British Columbia Teachers' Federation v. British Columbia, 2011 BCSC 469, [339], 85-86. The government also argued that in bringing in the legislation, it was exercising its power and authority to enact education legislation for the public good, its constitutional responsibility. It claimed, also, that the impugned legislation did not have the substantial impact on collective bargaining that the teachers alleged and that, even if the legislation did offend the *Charter* protection for collective bargaining, it is saved by application of s. 1 of the *Charter*.

138. British Columbia Teachers' Federation v. British Columbia, 2011 BCSC 469, [375], 95.

139. Janet Steffenhagen, "Striking BC teachers' union facing penalties," *Vancouver Sun*, 13 October 2005. weblogs.elearning.ubc.ca/workplace/archives/018735.php, retrieved 9 November 2008.

140. Andrew Coyne, "The strike as kitch," 12 October 2005, Andrew Coyne.com, retrieved 9 November 2008.

141. Without staff to provide instruction or maintain buildings, school boards went to court pushing for heavy fines. Defiance of the court order prompted Justice Nancy Brown on October 13 to instruct the federation to halt paying strike pay to its members and, later, fined the BCTF $500,000 for contempt of court. Despite the Supreme Court's action, teachers remained on picket lines.

142. "Teachers, government must find way to halt current madness," *Vancouver Sun*, 13 October 2005. weblogs.elearning.ubc.ca/workplace/archives/018735.php, retrieved 9 November 2008.

143. C. Brown, CBC-TV. www.cbc.ca/canada/story/2005/10/21/teachers-strike051021. html, retrieved 9 November 2008. In spite of difficulty securing an agreement, Vince Ready eventually cobbled together an agreement acceptable to both sides. Government offered teachers $40 million to harmonize salaries across the province, spent $20 million to decrease class sizes, and contributed $40 million to the federation's long-term disability fund. Even though the BCTF failed to achieve key goals related to salary, free collective bargaining, and working conditions, 77 per cent of the membership voted in favour of accepting the mediator's proposals.

IMAGES:

The Civilized World of City Schools

Nothing expressed the public's faith in its public schools more than the grand school buildings commissioned in cities and towns throughout the province. The first of the province's great architectural statements was the Central School in Victoria (later Boys' Central School), constructed in 1875 in an Italianate style. It was the first British Columbia school to be built of fine materials (stone, local red bricks, and sandstone dressings). Significant also is the fact that the small annex to the school was used to temporarily house the first Victoria High School when it was established in 1876, the sole school of its kind west of the Red River and north of San Francisco. **Courtesy British Columbia Archives H-06810.**

The gracefully proportioned three-storey Nelson Public School featured multi-gabled roofs and ashlar foundations when it was built in 1908, reflecting the public's belief in the great importance of schools in a mineral-rich city. **Courtesy British Columbia Archives E-09177.**

Raising and saluting the flag were commonplace events for many British Columbia schoolchildren in urban schools as the nineteenth century crossed into the twentieth. Kingston Street school youngsters from Victoria's comfortable enclave of James Bay are photographed here in 1902. **Courtesy British Columbia Archives A-09175.**

Girls' Central School in Victoria likewise illustrated the fine architectural design and attention to detail characteristic of urban public school buildings. The school's tranquil park-like surroundings were similar to those of elite private academies. **Courtesy British Columbia Archives H-06808.**

Pupils sowing seeds under teacher supervision to establish a Vancouver school garden in 1908. Such activities were deemed essential at the time by educational reformers interested in reconnecting city youngsters with an understanding of nature that appeared to be receding as people moved from farms to cities. Large school grounds stretching sometimes to five or ten acres provided plenty of space for garden development. **Courtesy City of Vancouver Archives CVA-660-642.**

The South Prince George School class photograph in 1910 reveals youngsters in front of a school building far more commercial in its architectural appearance than could usually be found at the time. This photograph records a rare instance where a school could be mistaken for a bank, land-title office, or some other commercial venture. **Courtesy British Columbia Archives C-08770.**

Penticton Elementary School built in 1913 in the Okanagan Valley set out in bricks and stone the high significance communities gave to schools during the Edwardian Era. **Courtesy British Columbia Archives I-22869.**

Burnside Elementary School in Victoria has been described as a "severe but harmonious structure" representative of an academic revival architectural style popular during the first two decades of the twentieth century. Designed in 1913 by prominent local architect C. Elwood Watkins (who would later design the impressive Victoria High School), the school's monumentality testified to the importance civic leaders bestowed on high quality school architecture and its potency in elevating young minds. **Courtesy British Columbia Archives H-06811.**

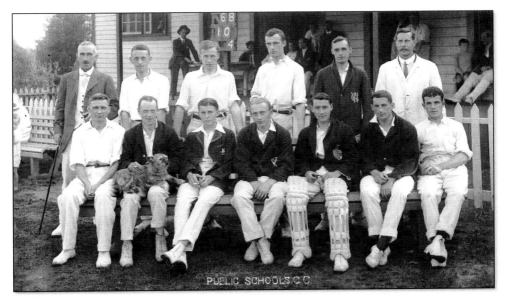

Keeping the "British" in British Columbia. A photograph of the Public Schools Cricket Club in Vancouver 1915 demonstrates the resoluteness of certain British traditions in far-flung corners of the Empire. Cricket and other British customs were characteristic elements of provincial schools and society well into the twentieth century. **Courtesy City of Vancouver Archives CVA-99171.**

Large communities in themselves: Early twentieth-century urban schools contained populations far greater in size than many small settlements found throughout the province. Strathcona School in East Vancouver (ca. 1923) was one such school. **Courtesy City of Vancouver Archives CVA-N11.**

Templeton Junior High School 1927 was in the vanguard of British Columbia schools to specialize in what is today known as "middle school" programs.
Courtesy City of Vancouver Archives CVA-N43.

A telegraphy class in King Edward High School (ca. 1930) suggests the close relationship between work and school in the senior grades, as well as the efforts of schools to "keep up with the times" by embracing new technology. **Courtesy City of Vancouver Archives CVA-99-3806.**

A model of architectural gravitas and elegance: Queen Mary School in Point Grey (ca. 1930). **Courtesy City of Vancouver Archives CVA-Sch N8.**

The British Columbia Legislative Buildings (ca. 1898) at the close of the Victorian Era.

CHAPTER 3

Disconnections at the Core

B ritish Columbia entered the twenty-first century with an educational system designed in the mid-nineteenth century. Almost all governance, administrative, and pedagogical structures that support the delivery of public instruction are archaic. Classes are grouped into schools and schools are defined by grades. Schools are organized geographically into districts that are locally governed, provincially sanctioned, and provincially funded. It is, in almost every respect, a system built for another age.

Overseeing this system is an education ministry that is actually "a ministry without schools." It is an organization that neither operates schools nor delivers school programs or services in any direct way, although it does oversee the K-12 system. Connections between the ministry and schools in the system are currently fewer and more tenuous than at any time in the province's history. It is also worth noting that the education ministry, its designation to the contrary, historically has had little to do with upgrading general levels of "education" in the province to satisfy economic planning or labour force requirements—those tasks have fallen to others.

One hundred and thirty-nine years after its creation, the institution of public schooling is defined by three interlocking bureaucracies that serve—intentionally or otherwise—as agencies for the prevention of change. Public schooling, for the most part, is dominated by an organizational triumvirate consisting of the education ministry, the BCSTA and the BCTF. Although rarely acting in concert, each of these organizations exhibits certain common characteristics. All are bureaucratic in nature, anti-visionary and unimaginative in outlook, prescriptive in behaviour, non-cooperative in manner, anti-technological in practice, and committed to the status quo. Nevertheless, all three organizations rhetorically embrace the idea of change as long as it requires no actual alteration to their own organizations, or to the existing school system.

This organizational triad also projects an image of schooling as an institution that is quintessentially "public." In reality, however, the system revolves mostly around meeting the needs of insiders—teachers, administrators, bureaucrats, and trustees. The ministry's primary clients are school boards rather than students, and the school boards' chief clients are, in turn, teachers' unions, district bureaucracies, and assorted interests, all claiming the status and legitimacy of "stakeholders." Students, parents, or the public can rarely be found near the apex of system priorities, or close to the mainframe of operations where decisions are actually made, despite torrents of verbiage to the contrary.[1] Editorialists and other writers in the national press have long warned British Columbians, and Canadians in general, about the uncurbed power of the educational establishment and the dangers of allowing a cabal of professionals to control the nation's schools.[2] Such calls of alarm since the late 1980s have prompted provincial governments across the country to increase opportunities for greater public and parental participation in schooling by creating parent-friendly school councils and by placing parents on provincial policy and advisory councils. The success of these initiatives has been no more than modest to date.

None of the three organizations that define the core of the public system appears interested in articulating a bold new vision for education in the future. No incentives exist for them to do so: all seem wedded to past practices through a mutual endorsement of the "One Best System" approach to public school provision, as historian David Tyack termed the singular and tradition-bound model of schooling that has historically defined state-supplied education in the United States and Canada.[3] In addition, each organization—at least publicly—subscribes to an official culture of denial that maintains nothing is fundamentally wrong with public schooling as presently constituted, as long as public coffers provide sufficient resources to satisfy annual professional and public demands. For every problem—pedagogical, social, or political—the solution is predictably and beguilingly the same, "just add more resources."

As Chapter 2 of this discussion showed, the structures and relationships that successfully governed and administered the public system for the first 100 years of its operation have proven ineffective—and in conflict—since 1972. Once-harmonious and effective governance and administrative relationships were undermined by six major developments: the post-1946 consolidation of school districts; the shift from local to provincial funding for schools; education's emergence as a political issue; the disappearance of strong leadership in the education ministry and elsewhere; the rise of special interest lobbies; and, finally, the BCTF's ambitions to control school policy and, thereby the province's purse strings. Each of these factors has contributed appreciably to the system's currently divisive state and to the turbulent character of educational labour relations over the past four decades. From any angle, the system now appears at odds with itself, a jumble of adversarial organizations and interests marked by discontinuity and discord. As it now stands, the system is fractured at its core and is directionless.

A Matter of Leadership

The troubled state of the schools and the malaise surrounding them can be traced largely to a question of leadership. Since the 1970s when partisan and special interest politics tore apart the old mandarin-managed empire of schools, the education ministry has become a shadow of its former self. Once the principal architect and driving force behind the system, as well as the chief advocate for schools, the education ministry has steadily retreated from providing either real or symbolic leadership. From the margins of the system, it now performs a handful of modest monitorial and regulatory functions in addition to its key duty as paymaster. Aside from supplying resources, it no longer serves as a point of reference for anyone inside the system. This should not be considered surprising from a ministry that now has little, if any, pedagogical expertise (as measured in staff with advanced degrees in education or the social sciences), a predilection toward regulation and accounting, and a coterie of bureaucrats recruited from non-educational backgrounds who fly no flags for schools.[4]

Reasons for the ministry's irrelevance are obvious. Over the past half century, the ministry has discarded most of the powerful policy and administrative levers it traditionally employed to direct the system—inspection of schools and teachers, district superintendencies, curriculum control, teacher education and certification, testing and examinations, standards, and some aspects of policy making. It is accurate—but embarrassing—to note that educational government's last great accomplishment was construction of the post-secondary system in the 1960s and that, since this time, neither political leaders nor the educational civil service have been able to articulate cohesive political, pedagogical, or organizational objectives for the schools, a clear mandate for their operations, a cohesive fiscal framework, or an approach to bargaining consistent with this framework.

Changing times and circumstances destroyed the latticework of relationships that once held school governance and administration together. Historical partnerships between educational government and school boards dissolved after the late 1960s as teachers' associations, aggressive advocacy groups, and soaring educational costs put new pressures on all levels of government. Provincial authorities pressed ahead into this new era without overhauling governance and administrative structures, believing that time-tested organizational arrangements and practices would suffice. Even the dramatic post-1980 expansion of the school's mandate into social and family domains produced no changes to the system's governance foundations, despite ample warnings that school operations were being stretched to new and dangerous limits.

In fact, no government throughout the twentieth century, nor any of the educational commissions they convened, saw fit to redesign a system of governance and administration first constructed in the mid-Victorian Age. Decisions by successive governments to prune their direct involvement in the province's educational affairs for the past four decades have led to confusion about "who's in charge" of schools and "who's responsible" for them. It has also allowed other organizations and actors in the system—most notably the BCTF—to step forward and claim that it speaks on behalf of public education as educational government retreated from the centre stage of school leadership. Such developments and others have meant that government's control over the public schools now appears to exist more on paper than in practice. Accordingly, the government's capacity to direct the system, and to determine its educational quality, is now at the lowest point since the public system was founded nearly 140 years ago.

A gradual but steady transfer of educational decision making from the civil service to cabinet and the premier's office over the past four decades has further undermined the capacity for leadership inside the education ministry. Ever conscious of their political masters, and the brief time-lines attached to legislative agendas, civil servants have grown risk averse and increasingly inclined to prioritize their activities according to perceived political pressures from in and outside government. An intrusion of politics into what was once a ministry ruled by civil servants has meant, not surprisingly, that educational government's activities have eventually coalesced around "advocacy issues" such as aboriginal education, special education, English as a Second Language, gender education, the prevention of bullying and substance abuse, as well as other potential political flashpoints. Suffice to say, equally important issues, the needs of mainstream youngsters, or inadequate program choices for high school students, for example, generate far less political heat and light and, therefore, receive considerably less attention.

Leadership at the political level of government has also been almost entirely missing. No education minister of recent vintage has been able to demonstrate a comprehensive understanding of public education's immense importance to the economic, social, and intellectual life of the province, or to outline a set of educational objectives that could be operationalized across the system. Education ministers have generally proved to be poorly informed about public schooling and reluctant to learn much about it. Certainly, since the time of Patrick McGeer in the late 1970s, no education minister has been capable of convincing British Columbians that it is essential to ascertain the quality of public schooling through rigorous testing, not simply because of the relationship between education and the economy but because testing remains the best way to ensure educational equity and opportunity for every youngster despite what the teachers' federation erroneously claims. As for other members of cabinet, few appear to know much about schools (regardless of party affiliation) or seem inclined to do much about them. Generally speaking, politicians realize the education portfolio constitutes a political minefield and, if possible, should be avoided.

The Waning Importance of School Boards

Leadership is in equally short supply at the school district level. Since school boards were granted authority to appoint their own superintendents in 1974 and 1980, the once-strong tradition of effective district leadership has largely disappeared. For the most part, superintendents have become captives to the whims of the boards who pay them, constrained by the vagaries of community issues and personalities, as well as the tight grip of contractual relationships with local teacher associations and support staff unions. The British Columbia School Superintendents Association (BCSSA) has likewise greatly declined in influence, especially since the advent of local control over administrative appointments. Once home to a cadre of strong-minded and outspoken educational mavericks, since the 1980s the association has lost almost all of its influence in government, the universities, and the teaching profession. Like the principals' association, the British Columbia Principals' and Vice-Principals' Association (BCPVPA), the BCSSA seems more directed toward serving the occupational and legal needs of its members. In terms of leading the province's teachers, or the larger system, to a new tomorrow, it is a spent force, every bit as disconnected from the K-12 system as the ministry.

School boards themselves, now numbering 60 since the last provincial restructuring exercise in 1996, are even more problematic and probably constitute the least effective component in governance and leadership. Concerns about the efficacy of school boards are not new in British Columbia. As far back as 1905, when the BCSTA was founded, the *Vancouver Province's* editor cautioned against giving too much decision making to local boards when he wrote: "the interests of the province at large are safer in the hands of a central administration than when placed in those of the municipal boards."[5] Although their sense of institutional self-importance has grown appreciably since the consolidation of small boards into larger governance units in the mid-1940s, the core tasks trustees traditionally performed in furnishing school buildings and taxes, negotiating salaries with teachers, representing local public interests, and establishing leadership and direction for district schools—the four main criteria for their existence—are now mostly performed by district staff or other organizations.

Today, most operating and capital expenditures associated with schooling are borne by the provincial government and supported by a property tax regime directed at equalizing contributions in jurisdictions across the province. Moreover, when the province stripped boards of their commercial and residential taxation powers some 20 years ago to stem spiralling school costs, they removed much of the political accountability boards traditionally shouldered for the spending they authorized. Since then, school board budgets have been largely divorced from the responsibilities of local property holders to pay for the district programs and services they receive. This has proven dysfunctional in several ways. For one thing, parents and other community members who see themselves as contributing nothing directly to the cost of operating schools are free to place unreasonable demands on the system, never appreciating that their demands impact other children elsewhere across the province.[6] Moreover, the more trustees spend and promise, the greater the popularity they enjoy with constituencies bent on having their interests served by schools. Such a relationship is not conducive to sound, or efficient, financial management. "The trouble with school boards as they exist," a *Globe and Mail* editorial declared summing things up across the country, "is that they are somewhat accountable in theory, but barely accountable in practice."[7]

Currently the provincial government oversees and finances a system in which many decisions about spending are made beyond its reach at the local level. Government efforts to monitor and audit the financial affairs of school districts and, in so doing, to demonstrate public accountability and value for public investment are routinely contested by board members, district staff, and by teachers inside the system. The political noise generated by this resistance saps time, energy, and money away from real improvements and, more often than not, leads to little more than finger-pointing exercises where government complains that school boards make poor decisions and boards complain that government has given them insufficient resources to do their work.[8]

A disjuncture between educational decision making and fiscal responsibility—a disjuncture provincial authorities have allowed to stand since the mid-1980s—has produced an annual educational passion play for the past quarter of a century. Year after year, from jurisdiction to jurisdiction, the liturgy rarely varies. On one side of the stage, boards vigorously complain that the schools are under-resourced, that the basic education program formula used by the province to calculate school funding is insufficient, that inflationary costs consistently outrun provincial grant increases, and that staff will have to be let go. On the other, provincial authorities point to annual increases in per capita grants, escalating provincial expenditures in schooling, various other injections of resources and, recently, to the shrinkage in public school populations. Such differences in views typically lead to games of political brinkmanship played out in local and provincial media. Little is ever resolved. Last year's stories will be re-cycled in years to come. From one year to the next, trustees reiterate their deep concerns about shortfalls in funding but usually decline to answer journalists' or government's questions about how increased expenditures on academics, fine arts, sports, and music actually translate into improvements in literacy, numeracy, or the other outcomes that schools pursue.

As to the matter of local representation, a history of extremely low voter turnout in school board elections, along with the influence of teacher associations over electoral candidates, has raised serious questions about whether boards, in fact, actually reflect the public's educational will, or simply serve as a platform for the expression of various special interests—all insistent on greater school spending, regardless of other legitimate public demands government is obliged to consider. "All residents may vote for the school board, but hardly any do," the *Globe and Mail* editorial continued, "[making] these large and barely visible institutions start to look a little like taxation without representation."[9] The Ontario royal commission on learning put it more bluntly in 1995: "Trustees are elected by a tiny proportion of the electorate, if indeed they don't win by acclamation. It might be embarrassing to discover how many constituents know their trustees' names."[10] In jurisdictions where school board elections are not tied to municipal elections, voter turnout ranges from as low as five or six per cent to 10 per cent of eligible voters.[11] Municipal elections in British Columbia are fortunate if they produce a voter turnout of 28 per cent but voters often decline to complete parts of the ballot relating to school board elections.[12] One recent by-election for a school board seat in a district outside Victoria produced a voter turnout of about two per cent.[13] Regardless of how people feel about the province setting educational directions and spending limits, one thing is clear: the province's electoral warrant to determine educational policies (as expressed in voter turnout, or degree of representativeness) is far stronger than that held by boards.

The question of whether or not boards encourage local interest in schools is another matter. District bureaucracies have grown substantially since the first major move to consolidate school districts in 1946. Such growth, however, may have served inadvertently to impede parental and public involvement in schools and may have stifled the ability of school-based groups to influence things at the school level. Bureaucratic size, specialized functions in district offices, and daunting numbers of district policies and regulations may, in fact, have served to deter parents and others from participating in educational decisions they once felt comfortable discussing in an era when school districts were tiny and integrally bound to the small communities around them.

Recent decades have also seen boards shorn of their responsibilities to negotiate labour contracts, a duty they shouldered since public schooling began. Difficulties associated with district-level negotiations since the advent of broad-scope collective bargaining in 1987—not the least of which were numerous strikes—were among the factors that led to a *Commission of Inquiry into the Public Service and the Public Sector* and, afterwards, to passage of the *Public Sectors Employers' Act* which established employers' associations for different parts of the public sector. Under the terms of this *Act*, the BCPSEA was created in 1994 to act as a full-service employers' association for the K-12 sector and to conduct bargaining on a provincial level with the BCTF. The shift to provincial bargaining freed boards from what was historically one of their most important duties. It has also added two new layers of organization to the governance structure of schools in the form of a bargaining agency that provides a full range of strategic policy and human resources services to school boards and, additionally, coordinates policies about bargaining and human resources in the educational sector with senior levels of government in the education ministry.

Finally, the track record set by school boards in providing educational leadership and direction at the district level can be described as nothing short of underwhelming. And this is not just a view from British Columbia. As the Ontario royal commission on learning straightforwardly declared: "Board agendas too often reflect matters that are light years away from what happens in their schools; anyone who has sat in on a meeting of a school board knows that it can be a truly surrealistic experience."[14] Generally speaking, school boards do not seem to play significant roles in improving the school system's educational outcomes. Much of the time, boards spend their time wrangling over "non-educational" issues of local governance, the "bricks, boards, and buses" side of schooling, along with debating other "input" variables. Many of their efforts appear mired in "process," their objectives are often fuzzy, and the arc of their decision processes rarely seems transparent.

While trustees argue at length about alleged needs for more resources and stir public fears about the unmet needs of "at-risk" children, they usually pay scant attention to the fact that British Columbia is locked in a fierce global struggle to prepare its citizens to compete nationally and internationally in a knowledge-based economy. Again, a disconnection is evident between provincial and local levels. Trustees remain focused on local matters arising out of a well-honed educational needs industry while senior government tries to ensure a province-wide standard of educational quality sufficient to attract intellectual and financial capital to Canada's west coast and, thereby, to assure British Columbia's social development and economic prosperity in years ahead. Looking backward, it is apparent that virtually all quality-directed initiatives adopted in public schooling over the past 30 years have been provincial rather than local in origin, including: the re-imposition of the core curriculum; the re-institution of grade 12 exams; assessment requirements in the early grades; introduction of an outcomes-based curriculum; initiatives to improve the performance of special and aboriginal students; and the development of Foundations Skills Assessments (FSAs).

After several decades of ignoring problems to do with local school governance, provincial governments from the Pacific to the Atlantic began restructuring exercises in the early 1990s that have substantially reduced the number of boards. Governments have justified shrinking the number of local governance units on assorted grounds, including increased efficiency, cost reduction, minimizing bureaucracy, democratizing local decision making, and integrating educational governance with that of other public sector services. The pattern of decline in local school governance is more revealing when viewed in longer historical perspective. In the U.S. alone, the number of school districts declined by 89 per cent in the twentieth century, from 117,108 to 13,506.[15] In Canadian jurisdictions, the situation has been much the same. Since the 1950s, the number of Ontario school boards has shrivelled from 5,700 to 3,200 in 1964 and, since this time, to 72. Over the same time, the number of school boards in Quebec (English-language, Francophone, and others) has fallen from 1,788 to 73; in Manitoba from 1,500 to 38; and, in British Columbia, from 830 in 1932 to 60 today. Such statistics suggest that the future for school boards appears anything but certain. A great historical tide of public indifference seems to be running against them, a fact well appreciated inside government.

About the "restructuring" initiatives of the 1990s, the Canadian Teachers' Federation (CTF) rightly noted: "The drastic reduction in the number of units of local government for education has been one of the most dramatic of all changes in Canada's pattern of government. And yet, it has occurred and is continuing with relatively little public concern or debate."[16] No doubt, the CTF's assessment was correct, although it stopped short of the mark. What the CTF did not explicitly say was that Canadians repose little confidence in boards, a fact that makes them politically expendable and, probably, likely candidates on a list of endangered institutions.

The great vulnerability of school boards today is that provincial governments are no longer reliant on them to supply the local infrastructures necessary to deliver school programs and services as they did when the province was comprised of rough trails and wagon roads. In other words, governments no longer need to delegate powers to boards as they did in the nineteenth century. Government regulations, policies, and information circulars can now be distributed effortlessly across an entire provincial jurisdiction through electronic and other means. The savings gained from closing 60 school board offices in British Columbia and centralizing educational operations at provincial or regional levels promise to be impressive.[17] And, although the presence of school boards allows senior government to divert direct public pressure away from provincial authorities, governments across the country have increasingly found the political stance of boards and their incessant demands for resources counter-productive and tiresome. Moreover, their very existence provides a platform from which teachers' unions and various other special interest groups can mount frontal attacks on government's educational policies and levels of funding, thereby undermining any semblance of cooperation and order. The current costs of retaining boards, calculated strictly in political terms, may already far outweigh their value.

Government and the British Columbia Teachers' Federation

Disconnections between provincial and local structures for school governance, and between legislative and administrative authorities in British Columbia, have been made much worse by more than 40 years of conflict between the provincial government and the BCTF. The BCTF's story in provincial school history—and the responses of various provincial governments to the federation's actions—has constituted a complicated and, at times, twisted tale. As Chapter 2 of this discussion documented, the BCTF experienced several stages in its organizational evolution. It grew from being an appendage to strong local associations to a centralized and powerful organization in its own right. Fifty years of finely balancing "professional" and "union" interests, along with presenting a moderate face to government and to the educational community, were discarded in the late 1960s as the federation assumed a more confrontational stance with the provincial government and with school boards. Since this time, strikes, walkouts, the BCTF's conversion to partisanship, demands to expand the scope of bargaining, countless grievances and legal challenges, the separation of principals and vice-principals from the union, as well as efforts to contest government's right to make public policy are all factors that have sharpened the federation's political edge and have dramatically reshaped the contours of employer-teacher relations in British Columbia.

Since the 1960s, provincial governments have proven anything but sure handed and consistent in their responses to the BCTF's economic and political ambitions. Mandatory membership in the BCTF, for example, was legislated by government in 1947 (on the understanding that the BCTF would not exercise the right to strike), rescinded in 1971 by a Social Credit government, restored by the NDP government later in the 1970s, rescinded again by a Social Credit government in 1987, and restored by an NDP government in 1993. Similarly, the idea of designating some areas of public sector work as an "essential service" was considered by W.A.C. Bennett in 1972, and again in 1974 by Dave Barrett's NDP.[18] Legislative amendments to prevent striking in the mid-1970s, however, did not include education in the list of essential public services. Education was included in 1978 after a protracted labour dispute involved Selkirk College and four school boards in the West Kootenays.[19] Education was later declared an "essential service" by William Vander Zalm and the Social Credit government, declared non-essential by Mike Harcourt's NDP, and still-later re-designated as essential by Gordon Campbell's Liberals.

Government has been equally inconsistent in its approaches to collective bargaining. From district consolidation in 1946 until the 1987 passage of Bill 19, the *Industrial Relations Reform Act* (formerly the *Labour Code*), negotiations between school districts and local teachers' associations were excluded from the *Labour Code* and bargaining was limited to issues of salary and bonuses. Despite the fact that public education had become a large public sector employer after 1945, the boards, as employers, had no duty or authority to bargain matters outside of compensation, notably the terms and conditions of teachers' employment, health and safety issues in the workplace, and disciplinary matters outside of suspension, dismissal, or probation. For reasons not altogether clear, government dragged its feet on this file for some time, no doubt preferring a status quo position to *Labour Code* changes that might prove more difficult and costly to manage.

When the *Canadian Charter of Rights and Freedoms* came into full effect in April 1985, it changed everything by affording British Columbia teachers the opportunity to challenge the constitutionality of certain sections of the *Labour Code*, specifically those that denied teachers the right to bargain collectively. Teachers filed a Writ of Summons in the Supreme Court of British Columbia, contending that certain provincial laws were unconstitutional under three sections of the *Charter*.[20] The *Charter* challenge, along with teachers' continuing demands for expanded bargaining rights, spurred William Vander Zalm's Social Credit government to introduce two pieces of legislation that would profoundly alter relationships between teachers, principals, and their employers. The *Industrial Relations Act* (Bill 19) granted teachers the right to organize into unions, to engage in broad scope collective bargaining, and, also, awarded them a limited right to strike constrained by conditions pertaining to the classification of education as an "essential service." The *Teaching Profession Act* (Bill 20) contained consequential amendments to the *School Act*, giving teachers a choice in belonging either to a professional association or a union.

Government's 1987 legislation proved immensely ill conceived in a handful of ways. First, its suddenness provoked an immediate and negative response from teachers, thereby perpetuating the divisive school wars that marked the public sector restraint era in the early 1980s. In setting out a choice between a professional association and a union, government also appeared to be vindictive in its efforts to destroy the BCTF's legitimacy as the teachers' organization and, once more, lost another battle in a never ending public relations war. It also sent a shudder of uncertainty through the staff of the royal commission on education who could not understand why government would introduce two substantial pieces of school legislation while a major study of schooling it commissioned was underway.[21]

Second, the legislation once again confirmed government's lack of understanding about teachers. Ignoring all evidence to the contrary, government presumed that teachers would choose a model of professional association over the protection of trade union status, despite the angry protests of the restraint years and the traumatic loss of some 2,000 educational jobs. The outcome of the teachers' vote was not at all surprising to anyone outside government: all 76 BCTF local associations selected the union model. Federation displeasure with the legislation also triggered a system-wide shutdown of schools on April 28, 1987 and, little more than a month later, prompted a general labour strike on June 1.

A third negative outcome was the separation of principals from teachers. Passage of Bill 20 set in motion a chain of events that finally resulted in the exclusion of principals and vice-principals from membership in the BCTF. The story of the principals' exclusion was a story in several parts. As far back as the 1940s, school trustees had argued that, as agents of boards, principals and vice-principals should remain outside the teachers' organization, thus first bringing into question the issue of BCTF membership. Although the principals' group had played a central historical role in the federation's rise to prominence, by the mid-1980s some principals had grown uncomfortable with the federation's politicalization and were expressing unease about the direction in which the organization was headed. In addition, a pattern of school strikes that had begun in the 1960s had disturbed principal-teacher relationships, as principals found themselves torn between allegiance to their teaching colleagues and loyalty to school boards and the youngsters in their care.

Historian James London portrayed the unfolding of events as the denouement in a political power play in which both the left wing of the BCTF and the right wing of the BCPVPA triumphed in getting what they wanted—the separation of principals from the federation.[22] Principals had historically provided some of the most reasonable and experienced leadership within the federation and, without their presence, the radical views increasingly embraced by the BCTF's executive officers were unchecked. Separation, in effect, exorcized what remained of the BCTF's political centre of gravity and its moderate traditions.

Expulsion of the principals also had profound consequences in many schools across the province.[23] Well into the early 1990s, teachers and teachers' representatives found themselves at loggerheads with principals on a daily basis over the smallest and most insignificant procedural and pedagogical issues, making the years 1987 to 1993 probably the most dysfunctional ones in provincial school history, at least at the school site level where programs and services were delivered—all thanks to legislation that was poorly considered and pushed through at the political level of government with little or no input from the educational civil service.[24]

Fourth, the 1987 legislation's hurried introduction did nothing to prepare school boards for the rigours of broad scope collective bargaining with teachers that would soon follow.[25] The results were both predictable and disastrous. School boards wilted under the pressure of a carefully coordinated system of local bargaining orchestrated centrally by the BCTF. In two federation histories the tactics employed were explained this way:

What emerged was a system of coordinated local bargaining. Locals were the bargaining agent charged with the responsibility of negotiating a collective agreement with their school board. The BCTF worked to co-ordinate all negotiating activities as well as to develop the Collective Bargaining Handbook, with model clause language on every conceivable provision that teachers might wish to negotiate. Local bargaining teams were trained by the BCTF and supported by staff assigned to work with locals. Additional staff were [sic] hired to assist and new policies and procedures were put in place to support the new bargaining regime including strike pay and assistance. On November 28, Kitimat teachers began a 10-day strike before successfully concluding an agreement. Eleven other locals struck in the first round and others mobilized to achieve their objectives that became identified in the slogan "Why Not Here?" We did well . . . [26]

The net result of coordinated local bargaining through three rounds was the achievement of comprehensive collective agreements that not only replaced the rights contained in legislation, but also enhanced and expanded those rights considerably. We obtained class size limits in contract, preparation time, paid maternity leave, tenure rights, [and] other workload provisions and professional autonomy clauses. And our salary increases were significant as well through this period . . . Collective bargaining had truly come of age for teachers.[27]

School boards were manifestly unprepared for the negotiations that followed the 1987 legislation.[28] Some districts mistakenly believed that long-standing relationships with their employees and their mutual concern for children would constitute sufficient foundations for amicable and fruitful negotiations.[29] Other boards depended on administrative staff, who in many instances lacked experience in collective bargaining. Still others employed lawyers and consultants as spokespersons in labour negotiations. By and large, few districts went to the bargaining table with the kind of expertise necessary to secure sound agreements.[30] London's history of the BCSTA bemoaned the paucity of assistance most boards received in undertaking their first broad scope agreements and concluded that boards saw themselves "getting burned with the 'whipsaw' cleverly administered by BCTF negotiation professionals."[31] Teachers, emboldened by strong and well-researched support services from the federation, outmaneuvered boards that were, in the language of the day, "all over the map" in the variety of collective bargaining approaches they adopted. In the five years that followed the legislation, the BCPSEA's Hugh Finlayson reports in a history of bargaining, 50 teacher strikes were called—about 16 strikes for each round of bargaining.[32] Between the turbulent principal-staff relations in schools, the unsettled labour climate among teachers, school boards, and government, and the implosion of the Year 2000 initiative, chaos reigned across British Columbia's educational sector from the early to the mid-1990s. Vander Zalm's ill-considered legislation in effect, gave birth to a bargaining model that would lead to process and outcome dissatisfaction for years to come, as well as continual uncertainty about how to make an effective bargaining structure in public education.

Fifth, Bill 20 created the BC College of Teachers, a self-regulating organization intended to certify educators and represent both public and professional interests. The college, however, soon became just another in a constellation of issues dividing government and teachers.[33] The BCTF portrayed the college's creation as a government effort to undermine the federation's influence in representing teachers' interests and issued a two-page circular to its members outlining why the federation did not want the college.[34] Eventually, the BCTF realized they had but two options—either boycott or control the college. They chose the later and BCTF-backed candidates filled all 15 elected seats on the 20-seat council. Today, more than 20 years later, a bitter struggle for control of the council continues with no immediate end in sight.[35]

Sixth, and finally, in passing legislation that permitted broad scope collective bargaining, government allowed boards to negotiate class size provisions, something historically protected as a matter of public policy—and something provincial authorities traditionally determined through levels of expenditure and was embedded in broader strategies for social, economic, and educational development. Class size, more than any other single factor, represented the largest economic driver in the public schools and, far more than a condition of work as teachers described it, class size was first and foremost a condition of spending for government. Small adjustments to pupil-teacher ratios (PTR's), today known as educator-to-student (ETS) ratios, produced momentous financial effects in operating and capital budgets, not simply in the salary costs of the teachers' cohort required to staff schools but in the costs of additional classrooms and schools, utilities and janitorial costs, along with the costs of training additional teachers.

For six years (1987-1993) class size, along with class composition, remained as bargaining items in collective agreements between school boards and local teachers' unions. From 1994 to 2002, class size was bargained provincially between the BCPSEA and the BCTF, save for the April 1998 Agreement in Committee struck behind closed doors between Glen Clark's NDP government and Kit Krieger, the BCTF's president. This agreement, conducted without the support or knowledge of the BCPSEA and its school board members, set lower K-3 class sizes, a move that meant hiring 1,200 additional teachers and underwriting $150 million in new funding for schools.[36] In 2002, as earlier discussed, class size and other matters to do with school organization were removed as collective bargaining items under Bill 28 and placed within a legislative framework by Campbell's Liberal government in the School Act, indicating that such matters had been returned to the realm of public policy where they resided before 1987.

Deep divisions in the philosophical and social views of British Columbia governments—notably differences between the socially democratic and labour-friendly NDP governments of Barrett, Harcourt, Clark, Miller, and Dosanjh and, in sharp contrast, the free enterprise Social Credit and Liberal governments of W.A.C. Bennett, Bill Bennett, Vander Zalm, Johnson, and Campbell—have provided an unsteady governmental platform from which to address class size as well as other vexing governance and labour relations problems that have characterized public education since the late 1960s. Restraint and the public sector upheaval it produced in the 1980s, along with the calamitous effects of Bills 19 and 20 during Vander Zalm's watch and after, occasioned the Harcourt government to convene a 1992 Commission of Inquiry into the Public Service and the Public Sector, headed by labour mediator Judi Korbin. The commission was directed to examine how demands for public services could be tempered by existing fiscal realities, and how the power of parties involved in collective bargaining could be balanced to prevent the kinds of settlements school boards had entered into after 1987 but could not afford to pay.

Korbin's investigation led Harcourt's government to embrace the idea of creating an employers' association for the K-12 sector, charging a newly-formed BCPSEA to bargain provincially with the BCTF, despite the fact that Judi Korbin had never explicitly proposed this and, also, that the BCTF opposed provincial bargaining.[37] Making matters worse, the Harcourt government imposed this new bargaining model in 1994 without any form of transitional support to ease the move from "multiple local agreements to a single province-wide agreement."[38] Strong differences remained on both sides of the bargaining table. Employers were resentful they had been stampeded into agreements they could ill afford during post-1987 negotiations and sought redress. In contrast, the BCTF was intent on keeping what its local associations had won and refused to consider concessions of any form, describing such things as "contract stripping." Not until May 1996 was a Transitional Collective Agreement concluded between the BCPSEA and the BCTF, but only with the help of a government intermediary.

Government intervened again in 1998, as noted earlier, when Glen Clark and the BCTF signed an Agreement in Committee that excluded the BCPSEA. This intervention spoke volumes about the special relationship that existed between the NDP government and the BCTF, government's disrespect for the BCPSEA bargaining institution it had created and, true to British Columbia traditions, suggested that a political "fix" was more decisive and quicker, and therefore preferable, to all others. A behind-doors deal between the NDP and the BCTF was important also for various other reasons. It damaged the fundamental labour relations notion of two parties bargaining in good faith. It granted teachers' unions unprecedented influence in determining how human resources were actually deployed in local school systems, thus greatly reducing the authority of principals and other educational administrators, as well as that of the boards they served. And, last but not least, it promulgated the idea that legislatively-imposed collective agreements could now become the new "normal" in labour relations. Since this time, with the exception of 1996 and 2006, NDP and Liberal governments have been obliged to legislate virtually every collective agreement into law. These actions hardly denote mature practices in modern labour relations.

A Public Relations War

Complicated governance and labour relations issues have been made even more difficult to resolve by the BCTF's subterfuge and posturing. For 40 years, the federation's leadership has deftly waged a public relations war with government, shifting from the position of "system critic" to "system advocate," as time, circumstances, and issues change—and as it suits the federation. Their litany of criticism is long—the institution of public schooling is badly flawed as a result of "teacher reductions," "increased class sizes," "funding cutbacks," "leaking schools," "the diversity of student populations," "the glaring inadequacy of the one-size-fits-all funding formula," "the misuse of standardized tests," "regressive policies," the "unilateral decisions of government and school boards," and a host of other maladies too lengthy to recount. "We live the reality of lack of resources every day in our classrooms," BCTF president Irene Lanzinger complained in December 2009, with more than a small measure of exaggeration.[39]

Ironically, no organization or politician across the country—including the highly critical former education minister William Vander Zalm—has been consistently as derisive about the conditions of schools and their capacity to provide a high quality education as the BCTF. In fact, it is fair to observe that the federation single-handedly pioneered the tradition of biting criticism that has dogged the schools since the 1960s.[40] Federation executives rightly brag about being "the most effective and vocal opposition the government faces" and government's "biggest public policy headache."[41] Year after year, the teachers' organization has taken great pains to warn the public about the system's glaring inadequacies, unmindful, it appears, about how this never-ending barrage of criticism has served to undermine provincial confidence in the public system and prompt the flight of many families to schools in the non-public sector. Given the extent of the decades-old and systematic neglect the BCTF has alleged, it somehow seems miraculous that the system has not altogether collapsed.

The BCTF's self-appointment as "system critic" has dressed the stage for a modern educational morality play the federation has carefully scripted and that regularly appears on the pages of the *Teacher Newsmagazine*. The narrative is simple and compelling, and the BCTF is cast throughout as an organization with a monopoly on virtue and social conscience.

Their story begins after World War I with teachers struggling against small-minded trustees who depreciate the value of good instruction but are eventually overcome by the righteous power of collective action. In a mythological past assembled by the federation's in-house and amateur historians, the Victoria school strike of 1919, the New Westminster strike of 1921, and the Langley salary dispute in 1939—all relatively minor moments in the grand unfolding of the province's educational development—are inflated in importance to depict a long history of struggle, the inevitability of conflict, and the historical importance of strike action.

These events, in former BCTF president Ken Novakowski's words, "served notice to government of our willingness to defend ourselves, our profession, and public education." Such reconstructions of "how B.C. teachers have evolved their collective presence," again to cite Novakowski, completely ignore the decades of relative tranquility that generally characterized the BCTF's relationships with government and trustees before the late 1960s, the pivotal role principals and inspectors played in the federation's development, and the interchange of personnel between government and the teachers' organization during the first 50 years of its operation.[42] These selective and inaccurate portrayals of the past suggest a labour relations history far more traumatic than it actually was, as well as an enmity with government and trustees that did not always exist. Moreover, these stories are not supported in provincial school histories, or in Bruneau's revealing chronicle of the federation's past.

In fact, Bruneau points out that the real source of historical drama or conflict in the federation's evolution was far more internal than external or, as he put it, "dissent and argument in the federation have always been strong."[43] Bruneau traced this to six "permanent disagreements," or philosophical fault-lines, that ran through the organization's history and fashioned its character along the way, including: a split between rural and urban needs and interests; a split between the needs and interests of younger and older teachers; a split between confrontationist and non-confrontationist approaches; a split between teachers who favoured "specialist" and "generalist" studies; and, finally, a split between teachers "committed to using public education to sharpen children's awareness of socio-economic injustice" and teachers who were more concerned with introducing "children to disciplined thinking in the traditional disciplines."[44] The post-1969 struggle with government, measured in full historical perspective, is therefore merely one of a larger series of conflicts, mostly internal in origin that, together, have created a combative edge now emblematic of the federation's public persona.

Altogether, the questionable reading of the past promulgated by the federation's writers seems designed to remind contemporary teachers about the BCTF's essentiality to their lives and to keep them in a state of psychological unease, forever fearful of a hostile environment comprised of mean-spirited governments and small-minded communities indifferent to the needs of teachers and, by extension, to the needs of their own children. Accurate or not, such a mythology no doubt assists the federation's executive in keeping the membership compliant, on the boil and, in line with a garrison mentality, ready to do battle at a moment's notice. The federation's highly selective view of the past certainly brings to mind novelist Peter de Vries wry observance that "history ain't what it used to be."

No wonder drumbeats from earlier engagements continue to echo in teachers' minds. No wonder British Columbia's teachers act in a far more bellicose manner than any of their counterparts across the country. Certainly, as the University of Trent's Andy Hanson has illustrated, teachers' unions in Ontario acted far differently by historically employing a strategy of quiet and reasoned professionalism to achieve improved salaries and benefits and to secure the right to strike.[45]

The roles in the morality play sketched out by the BCTF's executive changed appreciably in the post-1945 era as provision of school funding shifted from local boards to the provincial government (between 1944 and 1987, for example, the province's share of educational costs jumped from 27 per cent to more than 80 per cent).[46] With this change, the province replaced school trustees as the central villain. Since this time, school boards have been relegated, for the most part, to supporting actors, save for a few enlightened, sympathetic, and heroic trustees who approve all manner of educational spending and, thereby, demonstrate they actually understand what teachers and students need.

Thus, the geography of the story shifted from the local to the provincial stage where it has since remained. For much of the time from the late 1960s to the late 1990s, the provincial government is portrayed as the federation's new adversary. More specifically, the federation's enemies list consists of a roster of supposedly tight-fisted premiers such as W.A.C. Bennett, Bill Bennett, and, more recently, Gordon Campbell, who have seemingly remained oblivious "to the needs of children and the future" by refusing the federation unfettered access to the provincial treasury. These leaders are ridiculed and, sometimes, demonized for their policies that allegedly lead to "financial destabilization" and the "de-financing" of school boards. Plots and conspiracies abound according to the federation's high chambers, mostly aimed at advancing the interests of individualism and entrepreneurial capitalism over the social redistribution of wealth and opportunity that the BCTF claims to favour. In the federation's blurred vision, economic development and social development forever appear mutually exclusive rather than complementary.

During the past decade, the drama has transcended the old "white hat, black hat" stereotypes of yesteryear by allusions to governments controlled by darker and more sinister forces, notably "a new capitalism" that appears in the guise of "neo-conservatism, the corporate agenda, and, more recently, neo-liberalism."[47] "Under neo-liberal influences," a recent article in the *Teacher Newsmagazine* declared, "our global standing as a first-rate public education system was kept from the public. The unspoken message was that something had to be fixed, and decisive, harsh measures were required"—all, allegedly, "to advance the cause of privatization."[48] In this case, government was at fault, it seems, for saying nothing. Another *Teacher Newsmagazine* article purported that government has systematically undermined "labour, civil, and human rights on a broad front."[49] Or, as a similar article claimed: "The government's program of downsizing, privatization, and underfunding will carry on relentlessly unless we put a stop to it."[50]

Sometimes the BCTF's strategy of criticism is targeted toward what it sees as the agents of government, as in the case of former education deputy minister for the NDP government, Don Wright, who carried out a government-commissioned study of collective bargaining. In "Wright got it wrong," Novakowski takes Wright to task for recommendations that ostensibly sided with government, in effect condemning "the next generation of teachers to a potentially career-long struggle for equality and fairness at the bargaining table."[51]

Along with submitting to the "global trend . . . of neo-liberal market forces," federation writings claim government is also answerable for numerous other high crimes of state.[52] Testing youngsters to see if they are learning becomes in BCTF-speak "the current accountability madness besetting our schools." As former federation president Pat Clarke puts it: "Thanks to accountability and all its trappings we have a public school system that is evolving into a top-down, heavy handed, corporate-style, overly standardized mess," something that "will start to look like the shambles to the south of us, an over-managed, under-funded disaster."[53] Recently, the federation encouraged grades 4 and 7 teachers to "approach parents with a letter that encourages withdrawing their child from participation" in the 2010 assessments of achievement (FSA's).[54]

Efforts by government to focus system attention on student achievement, through the BCTF's opaque lens, becomes a dangerous intrusion, with administrators, as one teacher put it, having "the authority to stroll into our classrooms, to look around at what our students are doing, to ask parents what they think of us, to interview us, and to direct us."[55] Any notion of job supervision, or any challenge to the idea of absolute professional autonomy, it appears, is completely resisted by the federation. Again, in BCTF-speak, classroom time should be spent on "learning," not "tests." Concepts of accountability—or the government's responsibility to assure system-wide equity in learning—appear entirely foreign and unnecessary to the federation's vision of public education.

Amid a mélange of federation allegations and demands, several things are apparent. First and foremost, the BCTF has taken upon itself the fiat of moral goodness, and considers its views about education superior to all others by virtue of teachers being closer to children and classrooms than all other actors in the system. Accordingly, the federation claims that it is entitled to shape public and, therefore, fiscal policy and, because of its political influence, to negotiate directly with government at the highest level. It is also entitled, the federation maintains, to bargain full-scope conditions of work (including class size and composition), to withdraw services and to strike, and to bargain locally as it did following passage of Bills 19 and 20. Even if education is regarded as a vital service, the teachers' federation argues, in no way should it ever be deemed "essential." Such a designation would infringe on teachers' rights. Whatever rights students may have to an un-interrupted educational program seem beside the point, at least as far as the BCTF is concerned.

Politics and bargaining are forever intertwined in the federation's view. Glen Hansman, a member of the BCTF Executive Committee and the president of the Greater Vancouver Elementary Teachers' Association, put the matter in context in a candid 2009 article in *Teacher Newsmagazine*: "The political context is the bargaining context, and the bargaining context is the political context. We cannot separate the two, and we have the obligation of trying to ensure the best climate for bargaining—not make improvements for our members and for our students."[56] These are remarks that teachers, parents, and, indeed, the public may wish to reflect upon carefully.

Other contradictions are also evident. Although the federation claims to be non-partisan, it openly and unapologetically works on behalf of the NDP and has done so since the 1960s. Even before the Liberal government of the last decade was elected, it was working to defeat it. Such behaviours obviously do little to stabilize relationships with government. Even the NDP's historical efforts to accommodate teachers were abandoned when the stakes were raised beyond the government's capacity to pay, provoking a familiar barrage of BCTF assertions that provincial authorities are morally indifferent to the needs of youngsters. All-encompassing concerns with "children" and the "future" (as in "the future health of public education") typically mask teacher demands for improved salaries and conditions of work. The inadequacy of "learning conditions" is likewise publicly touted as a flag of convenience to ensure that "working conditions" find their way onto the bargaining table.

Academics and other educational writers have attempted to explain the struggle between British Columbia governments and the teachers' federation in various ways. Charles Ungerleider, UBC sociologist and former education deputy in the NDP government (1998-2001), traces the genesis of the conflict back to the days of Social Credit government and to "an ideological struggle between a teachers' organization animated by the spirit of social reconstruction through education and a government animated by the spirit of unfettered individualism and entrepreneurial capitalism."[57] Ungerleider's brutal simplification of the past and his transparent sympathy for the federation, however, disregards the myriad social, political, and economic circumstances that have shaped the behaviour of both government and the BCTF in different ways and at different times. His reductionist view that ideological differences explain much of the historical conflict ignores, among other things, equally destructive years of turmoil between the BCTF and NDP governments in the 1970s and the 1990s, as well as other contributing factors such as power struggles inside the federation, not to mention the vacuum in educational leadership inside government that inflamed teachers' ambitions to control provincial school policy in the first place.

UBC's Wendy Poole, a former high school teacher from the Maritimes, likewise provides scant intellectual traction in her analysis of the battle for control of public education.[58] The present-minded Poole entirely overlooks 30 years of educational warfare that began in the late 1960s, preferring to characterize the struggle as a recent and uncomplicated bedtime story of heroes and villains with teachers upholding the values of the social left and government representing the dark forces of the economic right. According to Poole, all is explained in the simple fact that the Campbell government "employs decidedly neo-liberal rhetoric and policy" while "the BCTF is vehemently anti-neo-liberal."[59] "Neo-liberalism," Poole contends, "arrived with a vengeance in . . . British Columbia with the election of a Liberal government" in 2001, a government bent on wringing "accountability" from the public schools, something she describes as "a consistent catch phrase of the Campbell government."

Oblivious to the traditions of provincial school history—and to the critical fact that public pressure on government for educational accountability is as old as the school system itself—Poole's shallow characterization of the dispute between government and the teachers' federation remains a dangerously oversimplified view. She presents an educational world comprised of only two actors and only two sides—those who unequivocally support the sacred trust of public education and those who fail this highly subjective loyalty-test on any number of grounds. These include reducing the size and power of the civil service, constraining spending on social programs, providing levels of school finance that allegedly do not keep pace with inflation, expecting school boards to balance their budgets, expecting schools to demonstrate student achievement, or increasing parental involvement in schools. In short, Poole's thumbnail sketch of events, and of government's many failings, manifestly neglects any serious assessment of the deep chasm of historical disagreement between the provincial government and the BCTF, or of the ever-shifting social, economic, and political circumstances that bedevil modern governments and, indeed, prompt calculated public relations and political responses from complex organizations such as teachers' unions.

A far more searching analysis of the political and social dynamics that shape government's views of the teachers' federation—as well as the federation's views of government—is Charlie Naylor's well-reasoned 2002 inquiry into "reconciling teacher unionism's disparate identities."[60] Naylor, a senior researcher with the BCTF, examines the ideological yin and yang that has occasioned "animosity between teacher unions and conservative but reforming governments" across the continent over the past 25 years in light of the precarious internal balancing act teacher unions must perform to equilibrate their "industrial, professional, and political focuses."[61] After carefully weighing the scholarly evidence about the pros and cons of "industrial unionism," "professional unionism," "social justice unionism," and "internal pressures" for union reform, Naylor suggests that teacher unions could profit by broadening the ways they present themselves publicly, thereby remaining relevant to "a newer and younger teaching population."[62] Sensitive to the "diverse" range of "educational, cultural, economic, social, political, and geographic contexts" in which teacher unions now find themselves, Naylor suggests "replacing the traditional 'shotgun' approach to the various teacher union activities (wherein everything's hit but nothing's covered) with a more targeted, cohesive, and productive approach."[63]

In the case of the BCTF, this would mean reducing the federation's "reactive" responses to government and the media, collaborating more widely with other educational organizations (including other unions and universities), and embellishing the professional focus of teacher unions, something Naylor claims that is currently confined to "a subordinate and an acquiescent place in union structures."[64] Such actions would no doubt reduce some of the political noise that surrounds public education and, perhaps, furnish some uncontested space for government and the federation to hold discussions. Developments to date imply that Naylor's vision of a new strategic profile for the federation has done little to dampen the enthusiasm of the BCTF's current executive for the old industrial union approach and the inevitable and mostly unproductive head-butting it provokes with government.

And, so, government and the federation remain imprisoned in a Catch-22 situation, consigned in effect to a twilight zone of acrimonious public relations marked by traditions of distrust and revenge on both sides. Suffice to say, opportunities to pursue sound educational policies, or sound bargaining policies, are slight when the fundamental calculations remain political and, more often than not, vituperative on both sides.

Accordingly, government refrains from articulating its support or faith in public schools—and remains disinclined to shore up a great public institution now in distress—because, de facto, this might be seen to endorse what teachers do and what the BCTF does. Alternatively, teachers and the BCTF cannot really get behind the public schools—a system historically well provisioned and well respected—because this might be construed as support for government's educational policies or, even worse, government itself. Consequently, government remains silent most of the time about education, never declaring expressly what it wants, or what its real intentions are. Bitter experience has taught government that no educational news is good news and that media silence is, indeed, golden. Not surprisingly, government stays off the educational skyline by choice and the resulting vacuum in leadership is evident for all to see.

In contrast, the federation is garrulous in expressing its criticisms, claims, and allegations: it suffers from a confusion of interests, defeating its own purposes—and those of others—by the extent of its accusations and the language of distraction it uses. The BCTF is a noisy and disruptive educational presence that appears insatiable: nothing, it appears, will ever satisfy its demands, or bring quiet to the public system. Genuine federation interests in the institution of public education, or in correcting the inequities in the province's social condition, are lost in a landslide of criticism and complaint that typically surrounds BCTF pronouncements. And, like the government, for all its efforts the federation seems unable to clarify in discrete ways the exact educational, economic, political, and social objectives it has for schools. Language, in the final analysis, is just one more in a series of differences that frustrates any kind of real educational accord between the BCTF, government, and the organizations that act on government's behalf.

Backing Into the Future

"History is the nightmare from which I am trying to awake," James Joyce's protagonist confessed despairingly in reference to the destructive consequences of Ireland's national mythology on its people. The same, unfortunately, could be said about school history during the last half-century in British Columbia, where various elements of mythology and reality have combined with equal ill effects. Disagreement about the past invariably precludes a shared vision of a future—and the cooperation it requires. Government—either in the form of cabinet or the education ministry—and the teachers' federation executive fumble about in their own distinct historical solitudes and have done so for some time.

Government, its organizational memory erased by decades of staff change and indifferent recruitment, is plagued by historical amnesia and unmindful of a time when the public schools were respected and much-beloved institutions. The federation, misinformed by its own revisionist and corrupted view of school history before 1967, seems likewise incapable of recalling an age of educational contentment when schools were recognized as the province's most important public institutions and when the school year was marked by more important events than running battles with government. Both sides bear the wounds of the past—government suffers from almost no historical perspective while the federation suffers from too much history, much of it wrong-headed. Distracted by the political reckonings that seemingly surround every decision, neither government nor the federation appears capable of re-imagining a future for the public schools, or re-invigorating an institution clearly archaic in many of its practices. Locked in the grip of the past, government and the teachers' federation, together with the province's other educational organizations, appear to be backing into the future with nothing more than a broken rear view mirror as a guide.

Good reasons can be found to change the character of the relationships that exist—for government and the federation. Various factors proclaim that public schooling is now a static and, probably, declining industry, and that some considerable urgency is required to sort out the system's structural and labour relations difficulties. Just as a "pre-public" era preceded the advent of the "public" era in education so, too, a "post-public" era may follow it. British Columbia may be on the threshold of this, or may even have entered it already. Following a century of stellar accomplishments, the great engines of progress and reform that powered the rise of the public school seem stalled. For the first time in its history, public schooling stands without a story to tell and without bold new ideas to move it forward. Arguably, the last idea to give the public schools a new sense of mission and momentum was the integration of special needs youngsters into regular classrooms 30 years ago.

Today, public education appears to be a stagnant institution, badly in need of both organizational and pedagogical rejuvenation. Even on its best days— and they are seemingly few—the public school seems to be without ideas or energy, an institution mostly preoccupied with maintaining the status quo and itself, not capable of playing an important role in the province's economic and social development. Sadly, no one associated with education seems able to re-kindle the spark of public schooling's noble and productive past. Anyone connected with public schooling should reflect long and hard on history's shifting tides and how current social, economic, technological, and demographical changes might re-draw the face of schooling in the years ahead.

Certainly, by any standard, the bitter struggle between the provincial government and the teachers' federation over the control of public education for 40 years has proven costly. The disastrous state of labour relations likely constitutes the single most serious impediment to educational progress in the province—and has done so for some time. Decades of conflict have created deep fissures in a province already historically polarized in its political and economic outlook—and have eroded the school system's energies. Parents, the public, and even educators have become exhausted and frustrated with the stormy state of labour relations in schools and the fact they never seem to improve. This strife has tarnished public education's once-considerable lustre and, no doubt, has appreciably reduced public confidence in public schooling.

Various studies and public opinion samplings since the 1970s have chronicled a mounting public unease with public education—a disquietude reflected in the steady march of parents toward non-public schools in recent decades.[65] A poll commissioned on October 7, 2005, the day the most recent provincial school strike began, indicated that more than half the families whose children attend public schools believed "the public education system is worse than the private system."[66] A spokesperson for the polling firm chillingly concluded: "this is not a vote of confidence for BC's public schools . . . parents' expectations are not being met by the public system."[67]

In light of the organizational warfare of recent years, some kind of governance and administrative restructuring for the system seems likely. Left unresolved, the federation's intransigence will eventually prompt a centrist or centre-right government to enact legislation that will break the BCTF's near-monopolistic grip on the delivery of school programs in the province. This may occur in various ways. Government could simply allow the college system to compete in the public school market by offering educational programs for grades 10, 11, and 12, thus lopping off some of the federation's high school membership and significantly depleting its fees and its war chest. Alternatively, government could simply encourage the growth of non-public sector schools throughout the province by making publicly owned facilities available to qualified providers, thereby expanding the landscape of private educational provision far beyond the Lower Mainland and Vancouver Island where it is now confined. Expanding educational choice province wide would have an immediate and profound impact on public schools and, by extension, on the BCTF. The clamour for non-public school spaces in the Lower Mainland offers potent evidence of parents' attraction to opportunities for greater school choice.

Or, government could simply remanufacture the entire organizational structure for schooling by regionalizing or centralizing educational operations, in the process eliminating school boards and, perhaps, reconstituting the system around individual schools governed by a school council and routinely supervised by a re-born provincial school inspectorate. The possibilities for reorganization are almost endless and the cost savings probably breathtaking. Such restructuring would also cut the "big government-big labour" nexus that has proven problematic since the end of the 1960s and, in so doing, remove a persistently annoying political albatross from around government's neck.

Changes in the way school programs are delivered likewise seems inevitable. Global transformations in the way knowledge is produced, distributed, and communicated, make it inconceivable that a nineteenth-century teacher-centred and expensive labour-intensive instructional model will continue for much longer as the exclusive model for learning, or that teachers will retain their status as the principal, if not the sole, providers of legitimate educational experiences. Federation arguments that technology does not improve instruction, or provide the "social" component of learning, increasingly seem passé in a world where ipods, ipads, iphones, personal computers, and countless other electronic messaging devices now define the social world and atomize traditional notions about community and sociability. Changes in work life alone will probably reorient the delivery of school programs away from the traditional autumn-early summer agricultural cycle toward new configurations and, possibly, seven-day-a-week service. Accordingly, the future for electronic or "virtual" schools appears far brighter than for conventional delivery systems.

Public schooling is also in trouble because public consensus about what schools can and should do has, in large part, collapsed.[68] Since the 1970s, profound changes in the structure of family life, along with increasing parental and student demands for specialized programs and services, has prompted the expansion of the school's mandate into the social domain. In customizing educational programs and services, the foundation on which the system was originally constructed was shattered. Notions of "special" and "exceptional" currently drive a system constructed nearly a century and a half ago around the idea of "common" programs for all children and explain some reasons for public uncertainty, dissatisfaction, and confusion about what schools can and should do. Twentieth-century movements to "individualize" instruction—albeit always an exaggerated promise at best—along with the post-1945 conversion of high schools into institutions offering "comprehensive" program choices and program streams greatly obscured the outcomes and "products" of the public schools, for want of better description. In contrast, standards of accomplishment in bygone days such as junior and senior matriculation, or even success in passing grade 8 "entrance exams" to high school, were milestones of pupil progress well understood by the public and professionals alike.

Since the late 1960s, however, a continual broadening of the school's educational and social mandate has saddled public schools with a tangle of purposes and responsibilities, sometimes at variance with one another, but each satisfying the expression of one or more advocacy groups. Public schooling has thus become an amalgam of competing and, sometimes, conflicting interests.[69] Evidence of the struggle for space in the public school's agenda could be seen clearly in the 2,350 written and oral submissions the 1987-1988 royal commission received, many of which were directed toward maintaining particular interests or so-called "stakeholder" positions.

These conflicting claims make the old-fashioned notion of state-supported schooling as an overarching "public good" more ambiguous and more difficult to define. Certainly, the longstanding idea of schooling all children together has been withering since the 1970s when an increasingly narcissistic culture began to celebrate individualism and redefine education as a "private good."[70] The staggering affluence of the second half of the twentieth century, characteristic of many parts of North America, has enabled, if not prompted, a flight from the public schools. Motivated by dreams of upward mobility and self-actualization for their children, middle-class and upper-middle class families—with public school teachers well represented in their ranks—have increasingly chosen options outside the public schools. The historical idea of making schooling "common" to everyone has thus faded in popularity in British Columbia as it has elsewhere. Despite the rhetoric voiced by the teachers' federation executive, education has become recognized as a commodity by an increasing number of British Columbians since the 1980s. A new education market has already made its presence felt.

The public school's importance is shrinking for other obvious reasons, most notably from significant changes in provincial demographics. The great educational bull-market of the mid-1940s to the mid-1970s has long passed and the system has entered a state of contraction. Relative to the overall provincial population, public school enrollments have steadily declined for nearly 40 years. From a high point in 1971, when nearly one out of every four British Columbians were enrolled in public schools, the proportion of British Columbians in public schools has shrunk to about one in eight.[71] The figures below clearly illustrate the changes in the provincial age profile (Figure 1) and the growing disconnect between school enrollments as a percentage of the provincial population and educational expenditures on schools as a percentage of the provincial budget (Figure 2).[72] Falling school enrollments and rising school costs are likely something that government cannot continue to ignore.

Today, British Columbia's school enrollment as a percentage of total provincial population is the lowest in Canada.[73] In the 2008-2009 school year, there were 56,000 fewer students in public schools than nine years earlier, an overall drop of some nine percent.[74] Public school enrollment is forecast to fall further from about 555,000 youngsters in the 2009-2010 school year to fewer than 540,000 for the school year 2010-2011. School enrollment will likely not surpass the 540,000-student mark again until 2017-2018, best part of a decade away.[75] Nor are future enrollments improved by the prospect of well-to-do families continuing to forsake public schools for the non-public sector, or to enroll in "virtual schools," which will erode the school's "common" character even further.

Looked at from another angle, the province's social character has changed considerably over the past four decades and is continuing to shift. In 1971, at the apex of the public school's place in provincial life, over 35 per cent of British Columbia's population was under 19 years of age. By 1993, slightly more than two decades later, the under-19 cohort had dropped to 25 per cent of the provincial population.

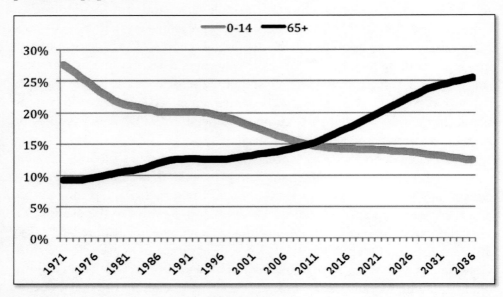

Figure 1: British Columbia's Population by Age Group, 1971-2036

This decline has put to rest a long-held belief that schooling would continue to be an infinitely expanding universe of provision. For many years, school history supported this view. Except for brief interludes caused by depression and war, public education evolved for nearly a century in a state of perpetual growth. Since the 1970s, however, few educators or government policy makers appeared ready to acknowledge that the great educational boom-years were over and that new patterns in family life, changes in the provincial population's composition, and changing patterns of immigration were substantially depleting the size of the school-age cohort.

Educators were equally reluctant to concede that public health would invariably replace public schooling as government's chief priority. Changing demographics as provincial and national populations grew older have overturned political priorities and forced government to redirect its spending.[74] Already some effects are evident. School closures of the last decade herald the first stage in what promises to be a larger shift toward a smaller system and, probably,

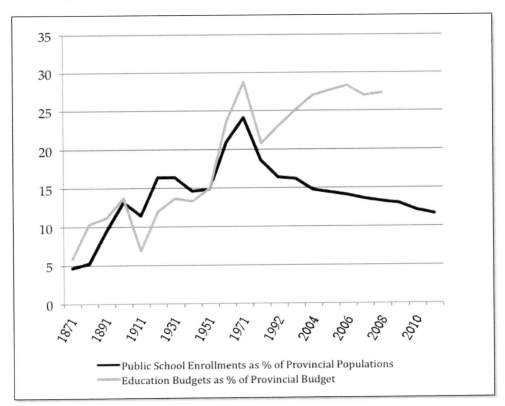

Figure 2: School Enrollments and Budgets for Select Years, 1872-2016

signal more dramatic restructurings in years to come. Put simply, public education has already entered a new phase in its development and is now in a period of contraction and decline. The fact that the percentage of youngsters attending public schools is now lower than at any time since 1911, a century ago, has sweeping implications for public schools. Among other things, it suggests that schooling is far less likely to be an election-determining issue. This, in itself, will significantly reduce the political influence of the teachers' federation. As enrollment numbers fall, and as the percentage of the provincial population attending school continues to decline, education becomes far less important as a political issue and, thus, far less consequential to government.

In summary, public schooling appears to be at a crossroads. Its institutional prominence in terms of population demands is declining, its political importance is receding, and its model of pedagogical delivery is under review, at least with many learners and their families. As to the years ahead, questions abound:

Will the influence of the three major educational organizations continue to dominate schooling, or will government allow new technologies, new agencies and other educational providers to reshape the landscape of educational provision and to meet the educational demands of a new century?

Will levels of government spending on public education continue to rise as school populations fall?

Will the complexities and frustrations of governance and labour relations that characterize the current system persist, or will ways be found to address the vexing bargaining and fiscal issues that now undermine public confidence in public education?

And, will government and the teachers' federation finally find ways to behave in a civilized manner, or will the discord of recent decades finally weaken support for old organizational relationships to the point that a new "post-public" universe of schooling will emerge?

Sooner or later, these are questions that British Columbians and their government will be obliged to answer.

Notes

1. Interviews with Barry Anderson, Victoria, 1 December 2009 and 1 February 2010.

2. See, for example: Jeffrey Simpson, "No time to waste in restoring common sense to our education system," *The Globe and Mail*, 15 May 1991, A 16; Andrew Nikiforuk, "Fifth Column," *The Globe and Mail*, 7 February 1992, A 24; Richard Worzel, "Time to take off the blindfolds," *The Globe and Mail*, 3 September, 1991, A 18; and Jeffrey Simpson, "Only one way to avoid giving Canada's education system a failing grade," *The Globe and Mail*, 16 May, 1991, A 18.

3. David B. Tyack, *The One Best System: A History of American Urban Education* (Boston: Harvard University Press, 1974).

4. Interview with Barry Anderson, Victoria, 15 March 2010.

5. James B. London, *The Dynamics of a Non-Professional Organization: A History of the British Columbia School Trustees Association, 1905-1980* (Ann Arbor: University Microfilms International, 1985), 58. Representatives from Nelson, Kamloops, Grand Forks, Ladysmith, Nanaimo, Victoria, New Westminster, and Vancouver met to discuss common problems and strategies (London, 35-36).

6. Interview with Barry Anderson, Victoria, 15 March 2010.

7. *The Globe and Mail*, "Good-bye school board," Monday, 28 February 1992, A 22.

8. Interview with Barry Anderson, Victoria, 15 March 2010.

9. *The Globe and Mail*, "Good-bye school board," A 22.

10. Ontario Royal Commission on Learning, *Report of the Royal Commission on Learning: For the Love of Learning: A Short Version* (Toronto: Queen's Printer, 1994), 50. Concerns about trustees' representativeness have also been raised elsewhere in recent decades. As one 1993 study observed: "Critics of the status quo in school governance . . . complain that local school boards have become too politicized and that they represent special interest groups, especially among the education profession, more than they do public interests. Attention, too, has been directed toward the costs of local school governance and its relevance, which some view as questionable." For the context of this discussion, see Thomas Fleming, *Review and Commentary on Schooling in Canada 1993: A Report to the UNESCO International Seminar, Santiago, Chile* (Victoria: University of Victoria, 1993), 64-65.

11. See, for example: B. Branswell and K. Dougherty, "Voters ignore school board elections," *The Gazette*, 5 November 2007; Henry Aubin, "Education minister should kill this bad idea," *The Gazette*, 1 December 2009; and Lance W. Roberts, Rodney A. Clifton, and Barry Ferguson, *Recent Social Trends in Canada, 1960-2000* (Montreal: McGill-Queen's University Press, 2005), 98.

12. Ballots cast as a percentage of eligible voters for local government elections in British Columbia can be found at www.elections.civicinfo.bc.ca/2008/reports/turnout.asp

13. Interview with electoral officer, North Saanich, 20 March 2010.

14. Ontario Royal Commission on Learning, *Report of the Royal Commission*, 50.

15. Thomas Fleming, "Provincial Initiatives to Restructure Canadian School Governance in the 1990s," *Canadian Journal of Educational Administration and Policy*, Issue 11 (November 1997), 3.

16. Canadian Teachers' Federation, "A Review of School District Consolidation in Canada," in *Economic Service Bulletin* (February, 1994), 1.

17. Simply eliminating some 60 superintendents, secretary-treasurers, and their staffs, say eight people per district at roughly $100,000 per person, would produce about $48 million in savings or more than one per cent of the overall operating budget for the system.

18. Hugh Finlayson, "A History of Labour Relations in British Columbia Schools," Unpublished manuscript, 2009, 18-20.

19. Ibid., 68.

20. Section 2, Freedom of association: Section 7, Everyone has the right to life, liberty and security of person, and the right not to be deprived thereof except in accordance with the principles of fundamental justice; and Section 15, Equality rights.

21. As a member of the royal commission's staff, I recall the feeling of dismay expressed by staff in our offices on Howe Street and the fear that such legislation would interfere with our investigation.

22. London, *Public Education Public Pride*, 386.

23. For a harrowing account of principal-teacher relationships turned sour in the aftermath of the 1987 legislation, see John Dressler, "Bill 20 and the Changing Character of the School Administrator's Role in the Schools of Cariboo-Chilcotin," Unpublished M.Ed. thesis, Victoria: University of Victoria, 1983). For an out-of-province view of events in British Columbia schools, see Janice Wallace, "The Work of School Administrators in Changing Times," www.aare.edu.au/01pap/wal10214.htm, retrieved 10 December 2008.

24. Three senior educational bureaucrats—John Walsh, Don Smyth, and Barry Anderson—confirmed that the details of the proposed legislation were entirely unknown to senior ministry staff until about an hour before their presentation to the legislature. Senior officials were never given a chance to critique or amend the content of Bills 19 and 20. They were simply allowed to read them for informational purposes. The legislation had been crafted, if that's the word, in lawyers' offices outside government. See also Fleming, "From Educational Government to the Government of Education," 232.

25. School boards, however, had considerable experience in negotiating full-scope support staff agreements at the local level with unions that acted independently from central union offices. But broad scope bargaining with teachers would prove to be a far more complicated undertaking.

26. Ken Novakowski, "Gaining full bargaining rights," *Teacher Newsmagazine*, Vol. 12, No. 6 (April 2000), 1.

27. "History of the BCTF," 5, http://bctf.ca/uploadedFiles/About_Us/HistorySummary. pdf, retrieved 30 March, 2010.

28. Finlayson, "A History of Labour Relations in British Columbia Schools," 18.

29. Ibid.

30. Ibid.

31. London, *Public Education Public Pride*, 407-408.

32. Finlayson, "A History of Labour Relations in British Columbia Schools," 19.

33. Ken Novakowski, "Teacher rights and benefits: Building on our past," *Teacher Newsmagazine*, Vol. 12, No. 1 (September 1999).

34. In April 1987, the BCTF distributed a document "Why Don't Teachers Want a 'College of Teachers'?" outlining the following reasons why the BCTF did not want the College:

    1. It will be divisive and disruptive. Education will be the loser.
    2. Freedom of association: Teachers' structure should be agreed – NOT IMPOSED.
    3. A college isn't needed. The job's being done.
    4. Cost and bureaucracy will be added to education.
    5. Professional certification: There is a better way.
    6. The college puts teachers in double jeopardy.
    7. All other provinces agree: A college isn't necessary.
    8. It won't work.

35. Janet Steffenagen, "College of Teachers calls for independent investigation," http://communities.canada.com/VANCOUVERSUN/blogs/reportcard/ archive/2010/04/06/ccollege-of-teachers-calls-for-independent-investigation. aspx, retrieved 5 April 2010.

36. Finlayson, "A History of Labour Relations in British Columbia Schools," 56.

37. Ibid., 45. The government's expectations for provincial bargaining were clearly articulated in the legislature by the Honourable Elizabeth Cull, the minister responsible for the Public Sector Employers' Council. According to Minister Cull, provincial bargaining would not solely take place between the employer's bargaining agent and the teachers' federation. "It is the trustees," Cull explained, "through the employers' association, sitting down with teachers representing districts from around the province that will make decisions on those issues that should be provincial in nature. Then, through the two-tiered bargaining system, teachers and trustees at the local level can make decisions about matters that are unique to their district." Cull further outlined the advantages of the *Public Education Labour Relations Act* by asserting that provincial bargaining: "will save us money;" protect "the rights of employees to free collective bargaining;" provide "greater stability" for students; "protect local autonomy;" create a "more balanced bargaining structure;" as well as allow for "responsiveness to local issues while ensuring that the major cost matters are negotiated provincially." Finally, Cull maintained: "under the new system, there will be a greater balance between the employer side and the union

side, and it's our belief that this will make collective bargaining more effective and that it will help to avoid the bitter relations at the local level that have become in many cases an obstacle to quality education in districts." http://www.leg.bc.ca/hansard/35th3rd/h0606pm.htm#11448, retrieved 1 June 2011.

38. Ibid.

39. Irene Lanzinger, "President's message," *Teacher Newsmagazine*, Vol. 22, No. 3 (Nov./Dec. 2009), 1.

40. See, for example: Noel Herron, "Vancouver's cuts in services," *Teacher Newsmagazine*, Vol. 19, No. 6 (April 2007), 1; Noel Herron, "Early-learning initiatives in BC steeped in politics," *Teacher Newsmagazine*, Vol. 20, No. 3 (Nov./Dec. 2007), 1; Noel Herron, "The Fraser Institute's flawed report card," *Teacher Newsmagazine*, Vol. 20, No. 2 (October 2007), 1; David Denyer, "Exorcising the Debt-Deficit Curse," *Teacher Newsmagazine*, Vol. 22, No. 2 (Oct. 2009), 1; Dan Small, "We say no to the FSA," *Teacher Newsmagazine*, Vol. 21, No. 4 (Jan./Feb. 2009), 1; and "Staffing losses threaten our top-ranked system," *Teacher Newsmagazine*, Vol. 16, No. 4 (March 2004).

41. Pat Clarke, "Why us—Again?" *Teacher Newsmagazine*, Vol. 16 (September 2003), 1.

42. "Executive Director Ken Novakowski's Report to the 2005 Annual General Meeting, 20 March 2010," BC Teachers' Federation, http://bctf.ca/NewsAndEvents.aspx?id=5042, retrieved 18 April 2010.

43. Bruneau, "Still Pleased to Teach," 81-83.

44. Ibid.

45. Andy Hanson, "Achieving the Right to Strike: Ontario Teachers' Unions and Professionalist Ideology," *Just Labour: A Canadian Journal of Work and Society*, Vol. 14 (Autumn 2009), 117-128.

46. ARPS 1971-1972, D190; and, British Columbia Royal Commission on Education, *A Legacy for Learners*, 153.

47. Kerry Richardson, "Neoliberalism," *Teacher Newsmagazine*, Vol. 22, No. 4 (January-February 2010), 1.

48. Ibid.

49. Ken Novakowski, "Wright got it wrong," *Teacher Newsmagazine*, Vol. 17, No. 4 (January-February 2005).

50. Neil Worboys, "Affiliation with the BC Fed: Now's the time to affiliate with the B.C. Federation of Labour," *Teacher Newsmagazine*, Vol. 15, No. 3 (Jan./Feb. 2003), 1.

51. Novakowski, "Wright got it wrong."

52. Diane McNally, "Paths to professional autonomy," *Teacher Newsmagazine*, Vol. 21, No. 6 (April 2009).

53. Pat Clarke, "A wooden stake for the accountability Dracula?" *Teacher Newsmagazine*, Vol. 18, No. 5 (March 2006).

54. David Halme, "A letter for parents on FSAs," *Teacher Newsmagazine*, Vol. 22, No. 3 (November-December 2009).

55. "Roaring 20s legislation: Implications for teachers," *Teacher Newsmagazine*, Vol. 20, No. 1 (Sept. 2007), 1.

56. Glen Hansman, "Failure to connect?" *Teacher Newsmagazine*, Vol. 21, No. 7 (May-June 2009), 3.

57. Ungerleider, "Globalization, Professionalization, and Educational Politics in British Columbia," 1.

58. Wendy Poole, "Neo-liberalism in British Columbia Education and Teachers' Union Resistance," *International Electronic Journal for Leadership in Learning*, http://www.ucalgary.ca/iejll/vol11/poole, retrieved 11 March 2010.

59. Ibid.

60. Charlie Naylor, "Reconciling teacher unionism's disparate identities: A view from the field," *BCTF Research Report*, Section 12, 2002-EI-01 (January 2002), 1.

61. Ibid.

62. Ibid., 4.

63. Ibid., 5.

64. Ibid.

65. The 1985 report, *Let's Talk About Schools*, clearly put the public schools on notice that British Columbians were not confident about the quality of public education and were desirous of expanding parental choice for school programs in and outside the public system.

66. "'Private Schools better than BC Public Schools'–says those with children in the public system," Vancouver, B.C., www.nrgresearchgroup.com, retrieved 12 December 2008.

67. Ibid.

68. Since the mid-1970s, governments in many jurisdictions have appeared confused in the philosophical approaches they have taken to the provision of public sector programs and services, including education. See Thomas Fleming, "Canadian School Policy in Liberal and Post-Liberal Eras: Historical Perspectives on the Changing Social Context of Schooling, 1846-1990," *Journal of Educational Policy*, Vol. 6, No. 2 (1991), 183-199.

69. The competition is not just among special interest groups wishing to see certain programs and services maintained in schools. Even in its economic and social functions, the public school is pulled in different directions. For working parents, schools represent an indispensable custodial service—and one essential to the family economy—quite apart from their educational mission. Colleges and universities likewise rely on schools to act as "free" screening agencies that select students for the post-secondary sector. To teachers and other unionized workers,

schools represent a permanent and well-paid source of public sector employment. Similarly, to government departments charged with directing a stream of health and other services to children, schools serve as agencies of great social convenience where programs can be efficiently delivered. And, finally, in countless communities around British Columbia, school organizations are vital customers that purchase an array of goods and services from local businesses, in effect institutions that ensure the province-wide distribution of public revenues. In short, a constellation of expectations is attached to public schools.

70. A changing culture was well documented in Christopher Lasch, *The Cult of Narcissism: American Life in an Age of Diminishing Expectations* (New York: W.W. Norton, 1979).

71. Data obtained from BC Stats (07/07) and from BCstats.gov.bc.ca/Data/pop/pop/agingpop/pdf, 20 December 2009.

72. Projected on the basis of recent year-to-year increases. In chronological order, data are derived from: British Columbia Department of Education, *One Hundred Years*, 68 and 90; M.C. Urquhart and K.A.H. Buckley, *Historical Statistics of Canada* (Ottawa: Statistics Canada and the Social Science Federation of Canada, 1983), 588-589; BC Progress Board, *Working Together to Improve Performance 2006* (Vancouver: BC Progress Board, 2006), 4; British Columbia Ministry of Education, *2008/2009 Summary of Key Information*, 2 and 3; Population statistics, bcstats.gov.bc.ca/data/pop/pop/BCPop.asp; and financial data from http://www.fin.gov.bc.ca/pubs.htm. Special thanks to Jerry Mussio for help in preparing this figure.

73. BC Progress Board, *Working Together to Improve Performance: Preparing BC's Public Education System for the Future* (Vancouver: BC Progress Board, 2006), 36.

74. British Columbia Ministry of Education, 2008/2009 *Summary of Key Information*, at www.bced.gov.bc.ca/reporting/docs/ski09.pdf, 2, accessed online 22 December, 2009.

75. Ibid., 3.

Bibliography

Adams, Joan and Becky Thomas. *Floating Schools and Frozen Inkwells: The One-Room Schools of British Columbia*. Vancouver: Harbour Publishing, 1985.

Anderson, Barry. "Financial Management of Education in British Columbia: A Background Paper." British Columbia Ministry of Education, 1984.

Andrews, Gerry. *Metis Outpost. Memoirs of the First Schoolmaster at the Metis Settlement of Kelly Lake, B. C., 1923-1925*. Victoria: Published by the author, 1985.

Ashworth, Mary. *The Forces Which Shaped Them: A History of the Education of Minority Group Children in British Columbia*, Vancouver: New Star Books, 1979.

Bancroft, Hubert Howe. *History of British Columbia, 1792-1887: The Works of Hubert Howe Bancroft, Vol. XXXII*. San Francisco: The History Company, 1887.

Barman, Jean. "Growing Up British in British Columbia: The Vernon Preparatory School, 1914-1946." In J. Donald Wilson and David C. Jones (Eds.). *Schooling and Society in Twentieth Century British Columbia*. Calgary: Detselig, 1980, 119-138.

-------- "Marching to Different Drummers: Public Education and Private Schools in British Columbia, 1900-1950." *British Columbia Historical News*. Vol. 14, No. 1 (Fall 1980): 2-11.

--------- *Growing Up British in British Columbia: Boys in Private School*. Vancouver: University of British Columbia Press, 1984.

-------- "Transfer, Imposition, or Consensus. The Emergence of Educational Structures in Nineteenth-Century British Columbia." In Nancy M. Sheehan, J. Donald Wilson, and David C. Jones (Eds.). *Schools in the West: Essays in Canadian Educational History*. Calgary: Detselig, 1986, 241-264.

-------- "Birds of Passage or Early Professionals? Teachers in Late-Nineteenth Century British Columbia." *Historical Studies in Education/Revue d'histoire de l'éducation*. Vol. 2, No. 1 (Spring 1990): 17-36.

-------- *The West Beyond the West: A History of British Columbia*. Toronto: University of Toronto Press, 1991.

--------- "Pioneer Teachers of British Columbia." *British Columbia Historical News*. Vol. 25, No. 1 (Winter 1991-1992): 15-18.

-------- "British Columbia's Pioneer Teachers." In Jean Barman, Neil Sutherland, and J. Donald Wilson (Eds.). *Children, Teachers and Schools in the History of British Columbia*. Calgary: Detselig, 1995, 189-208.

-------- and Neil Sutherland. "Royal Commission Retrospective." In Jean Barman, Neil Sutherland, and J. Donald Wilson (Eds.). *Children, Teachers and Schools in the History of British Columbia*. Calgary: Detselig, 1995, 411-426.

--------, Neil Sutherland, and J. Donald Wilson (Eds.). *Children, Teachers and Schools in the History of British Columbia*. Calgary: Detselig, 1995, 411-426.

Bloch, Mark. *The Historian's Craft*. Manchester: Manchester University Press, 1954.

Boggis, Steve. *A History of Public Schools in Richmond, 1877-1979*. Richmond: Richmond School Board, 1979.

British Columbia Department of Education. *One Hundred Years: Education in British Columbia*. Victoria: Queen's Printer, 1972.

British Columbia Provincial School Review Committee. *Let's Talk About Schools: A Report to the Minister of Education and the People of British Columbia*. Victoria: British Columbia Ministry of Education, 1985.

British Columbia Royal Commission on Education. *A Legacy for Learners*. Victoria: Queen's Printer, 1988.

British Columbia Teachers' Federation. *The Report of the Commission on Education of the British Columbia Teachers' Federation: Involvement—The Key to Better Schools*. Vancouver: British Columbia Teachers' Federation, 1968.

Brown, Helen. "Financing Nanaimo Schools in the 1890s: Local Resistance to Provincial Control." In Thomas Fleming (Ed.). *School Leadership: Essays on the British Columbia Experience, 1872-1995*. Mill Bay: Bendall Books, 2001, 199-220.

Bruneau, William. "'Still Pleased to Teach:' A Thematic Study of the British Columbia Teachers' Federation, 1917-1978." Unpublished paper, University of British Columbia, 1978.

Calam, John. "Culture and Credentials: A Note on Late Nineteenth-Century Teacher Certification in British Columbia." *British Columbia Historical News*. Vol. 14, No. 1 (Fall 1980): 12-15.

-------- "Teaching the Teachers: Establishment and Early Years of B.C. Provincial and Normal Schools." In Nancy M. Sheehan, J. Donald Wilson, and David C. Jones (Eds.). *Schools in the West: Essays in Canadian Educational History*. Calgary: Detselig, 1986, 75-98.

-------- (Ed.). *Alex Lord's British Columbia: Recollections of a Rural School Inspector, 1915-1936*. Vancouver: University of British Columbia Press, 1991.

---------- "Teaching Teachers on Campus: Initial Moves and the Search for UBC's First Professor of Education." *Historical Studies in Education/Revue d'histoire de l'éducation*. Vol. 6, No. 2 (Fall 1994): 117-200.

-------- "Alex Lord: The School Inspector's World, 1915-1936." In Thomas Fleming (Ed.). *School Leadership: Essays on the British Columbia Experience, 1872-1995*. Mill Bay: Bendall Books, 2001, 79-98.

---------- "The Principalship: Reflections on the Past." In Thomas Fleming (Ed.). *School Leadership: Essays on the British Columbia Experience, 1872-1995*. Mill Bay: Bendall Books 2001, 287-320.

---------- and Thomas Fleming. *British Columbia Schools and Society: Commissioned Papers, Volume 1*. Victoria: Queen's Printer, 1988.

Cameron, Maxwell A. *Report of the Commission of Inquiry into Educational Finance*. Victoria: King's Printer, 1945.

Carlin, E.M. "Excerpts of Interviews with Deputy Ministers of Education, 1970-1984." Unpublished report, University of British Columbia, 1984.

Chalmers, John C. *Schools of the Foothills Province: The Story of Public Education in Alberta*. Toronto: University of Toronto Press, 1967.

Chant, S.N.F., J.E. Liersch, and R.P. Walrod. *Report of the Royal Commission on Education*. Victoria: Queen's Printer, 1960.

Child, Alan H. "'A Little Tempest:' Public Reaction to the Formation of a Large Educational Unit in the Peace River District of British Columbia." *BC Studies*. No. 16 (Winter 1972-73): 57-70.

-------- "Herbert S. King, Administrative Idealist." In Robert Patterson, John W. Chalmers, and John Friesen (Eds.). *Profiles of Canadian Educators*. Toronto: DC Heath, 1974, 313-316.

Cochrane, Jean. *The One-Room School in Canada*. Toronto: Fitzhenry and Whiteside, 1981.

Cocking, Clive (Ed.). *Fond Memories: Recollections of Britannia High School's First 75 Years, 1908-1983*. Vancouver: Britannia High School Diamond Jubilee Reunion Committee, 1983.

Conway, C.B. *Pressure Points and Growing Pains in Beautiful B.C.: Informal Paper*. Toronto: Ontario Institute for Studies in Education, 1971.

Cottingham, Mollie, "Growing Pains: The Story of the Growth of Education in a Booming Province." *British Columbia Parent-Teacher*. Vol. 24, No. 1 (October-November 1957): 12-13.

Crawley, Mike. *Schoolyard Bullies: Messing with British Columbia's Education System*. Victoria: Orca Book Publishers, 1995.

Dennison, Robert. "A Study of the Prince George Citizen, 1957-1961: Editorial Reaction to Education and the Chant Commission on Education (1960)." Unpublished major paper in Social and Educational Studies, University of British Columbia, 1984.

Downey, L.W. "The Aid-to-Independent-Schools Movement in British Columbia." In Nancy M. Sheehan, J. Donald Wilson, and David C. Jones (Eds.). *Schools in the West: Essays in Canadian Educational History.* Calgary: Detselig, 1986, 305-323.

Dressler, John. "Bill 20 and the Changing Character of the School Administrator's Role in the Schools of Cariboo-Chilcotin." Unpublished M.Ed. thesis, University of Victoria, 1993.

Dunae, Patrick A. *The School Record: A Guide to Government Archives Relating to Education in British Columbia, 1852-1946.* Victoria: Ministry of Government Services, 1992.

-------- "John Jessop." *Dictionary of Canadian Biography.* XIII (1994): 511-516.

-------- "School Records and Education Anniversaries." *British Columbia Historical News.* Vol. 35, No. 1 (Winter 2001/2002): 23.

Dunn, Timothy. "The Rise of Mass Public Schooling in British Columbia, 1900-1929." In J. Donald Wilson and David C. Jones (Eds.). *Schooling and Society in Twentieth Century British Columbia.* Calgary: Detselig, 1980, 23-52.

Eberwein, David. "Teacher Collective Bargaining in B.C. Perspectives on the Vancouver School District." Unpublished M.Ed. thesis, Simon Fraser University, 1995.

Finlayson, Hugh. "A History of Labour Relations in British Columbia Schools." Unpublished manuscript, 2009.

Fleming, Thomas. "'Our Boys in the Field': School Inspectors, Superintendents, and the Changing Character of School Leadership in British Columbia." In Nancy M. Sheehan, J. Donald Wilson, and David C. Jones (Eds.). *Schools in the West: Essays in Canadian Educational History.* Calgary: Detselig, 1986, 285-304.

-------- "In the Imperial Age and After: Patterns of British Columbia School Leadership and the Institution of the Superintendency, 1872-1988." *BC Studies.* No. 81 (Spring 1989): 50-76.

-------- "Historical Strategies for Solving the Problems of Small Schools: Reflections on the Royal Commission of 1988 and Other British Columbia Commissions of Enquiry." *BC Historical News.* Vol. 24, No. 4 (1990): 12-15.

-------- "Letters from Headquarters: Alexander Robinson and the British Columbia Education Office, 1899-1919." *Journal of Educational Administration and Foundations.* Vol. 10, No. 2 (December 1995): 11-38.

-------- "Provincial Initiatives to Restructure Canadian School Governance in the 1990s." *Canadian Journal of Educational Administration and Policy,* Issue 11 (October 1997): 1-30.

-------- "British Columbia Principals: Scholar-Teachers and Administrative Amateurs in Victorian and Edwardian Eras, 1872-1918." In Thomas Fleming (Ed.). *School Leadership: Essays on the British Columbia Experience, 1872-1995.* Mill Bay: Bendall Books, 2001, 249-286.

-------- "From Educational Government to the Government of Education: The Decline and Fall of the British Columbia Ministry of Education, 1972-1996." *Historical Studies in Education/Revue d'histoire de l'éducation.* Vol. 13, No. 2 (Fall/automne 2003): 210-236.

-------- and Madge Craig. "The Anatomy of a Resignation: Margaret Strong and the New Westminster School Board, 1911-1913." *Educational Administration and Foundations Journal.* Vol. 5 (June 1990): 7-23.

-------- and Carolyn Smyly. "Beyond Hope, Past Redemption: The Lottie Bowron Story." *The Beaver.* Vol. 71, No. 2 (1991): 33-41.

-------- and Tara Toutant. "Redefining the Time of Transition: Junior High and Middle School Movements in British Columbia, 1925-1994." *Education Canada.* (Autumn 1995): 30-49.

-------- and Carolyn Smyly. "The Diary of Mary Williams, A Cameo of Rural Schooling in British Columbia, 1922-1924." In Jean Barman, Neil Sutherland, and J. Donald Wilson (Eds.). *Children, Teachers and Schools in the History of British Columbia,* Calgary: Detselig, 1995, 259-284.

-------- and B. Hutton. "School Boards, District Consolidation, and Educational Governance in British Columbia, 1872-1995." *Canadian Journal of Educational Administration and Policy.* Issue 10 (January 1997): 1-22.

-------- and Alastair Glegg. "Teaching to the Test or Testing to Teach? Educational Assessment in British Columbia, 1872-2002." *Historical Studies in Education,* Vol. 16, No. 1 (2004): 115-137.

-------- and Helen Raptis. "Government's Paper Empire: Historical Perspectives on Measuring Student Achievement in British Columbia Schools, 1872-1999." *Journal of Administration and History.* Vol. 37, No. 2 (September 2005): 173-202.

Franklin, Douglas and John Fleming. *Early School Architecture in British Columbia: An Architectural History and Inventory of Buildings to 1930.* Victoria: Heritage Conservation Branch, 1980.

Giles, Valerie. *Annotated Bibliography of Education History in British Columbia: A Royal British Columbia Museum Technical Report.* Victoria: Royal British Columbia Museum, 1992.

Gillie, Bernard C. "When It Was Easy to Go Teaching." *Historical News* 29, 2 (1996): 19-22.

Glanville, Alice. *Schools of the Boundary: 1891-1991.* Merritt: Sonoteck Publishing, 1991.

Glegg, Alastair. "Changing Public Attitudes to Government Initiatives in British Columbia Schools, 1865-1995." In Thomas Fleming (Ed.). *School Leadership: Essays on the British Columbia Experience, 1872-1995.* Mill Bay: Bendall Books, 2001, 405-424.

--------- "Schools in the City: The Effects of Increasing Urbanization on Education in Victoria, British Columbia, 1920-1929." *Journal of Educational Administration and History.* Vol. 33, No. 2 (July 2001): 73-86.

Goldman, Paul. "Jump-Starting Educational Reform: Implementing British Columbia's Comprehensive School Act." *Annual Meeting of the University Council for Educational Administration, Pittsburg, PA, October 26-28, 1990.*

Gosbee, Chuck and Leslie Dyson (Eds.). *"Glancing Back." Reflections and Anecdotes on Vancouver Public Schools.* Vancouver: Vancouver School Board, 1988.

Hanson, Andy. "Achieving the Right to Strike: Ontario Teachers' Unions and Professionalist Ideology." *Just Labour: A Canadian Journal of Work and Society.* Vol. 14 (Autumn 2009): 117-128.

Hawthorne, Dan. "British Columbia by Design: The Sullivan Royal Commission in Historical Perspective." *Journal of Canadian Studies.* Vol. 25, No. 3 (Fall 1990): 140-159.

Hindle, George. *The Educational System of British Columbia: An Appreciative and Critical Estimate of the Educational System of the Mountain Province.* Trail: Trail Printing and Publishing Co., 1918.

Johnson, F. Henry. *A History of Public Education in British Columbia.* Vancouver: University of British Columbia Publications Centre, 1964.

-------- *John Jessop. Goldseeker and Educator: Founder of the British Columbia School System.* Vancouver: Mitchell Press, 1971.

-------- "The Ryersonian Influence on the Public School System of British Columbia." *BC Studies.* No. 10 (1971): 27-34.

-------- "V. Revolt: The RTA in British Columbia—A History of Public Education in British Columbia Amended Manuscript." University of British Columbia Special Collections (ca. 1975).

Jones, David C. "'We cannot allow it to be run by those who do not understand education:' Agricultural Schooling in the Twenties." *BC Studies.* No. 39 (Autumn 1978): 30-60.

-------- "Creating Rural-Minded Teachers: The British Columbia Experience." In David C. Jones, Nancy M. Sheehan, and Robert M. Stamp (Eds.). *Shaping the Schools of the Canadian West.* Calgary: Detselig, 1979, 155-176.

-------- "The Strategy of Rural Enlightenment: Consolidation in Chilliwack." In David C. Jones, Nancy M. Sheehan, and Robert M. Stamp (Eds.). *Shaping the Schools of the Canadian West.* Calgary: Detselig, 1979, 136-154.

---------- "The *Zeitgeist* of Western Settlement: Education and the Myth of the Land." In J. Donald Wilson and David C. Jones (Eds.). *Schooling and Society in Twentieth-Century British Columbia*. Calgary: Detselig, 1980, 71-89.

----------, Nancy M. Sheehan, and Robert M. Stamp (Eds.). *Shaping the Schools of the Canadian West*. Calgary: Detselig, 1979.

Kilian, Crawford. *School Wars: The Assault on B.C. Education*. Vancouver: New Star Books, 1985.

Kindling the Spark: The Era of One-Room Schools. An Anthology of Teachers' Experiences. Published in Celebration of the 50th Anniversary of the British Columbia Retired Teachers' Association. Vancouver: BCRTA, 1996.

Kuehn, Larry. "'Nobody Voted for That': The Attack on Public Education in B.C." *Our Schools/Ourselves* Volume 11, No. 3 (Spring 2002): 51-62.

Lasch, Christopher. *The Cult of Narcissism: American Life in an Age of Diminishing Expectations*. New York: W.W. Norton, 1979.

London, James B. *The Dynamics of a Non-Professional Organization: A History of the British Columbia School Trustees Association, 1905-1980*. Ann Arbor: University Microfilms International, 1985.

---------- *Public Education Public Pride: The Centennial History of the British Columbia School Trustees Association*. Vancouver: British Columbia School Trustees Association, 2005.

Lortie, Dan C. *Schoolteacher: A Sociological Study*. Chicago: University of Chicago Press, 1975.

MacLaurin, Donald L. "Education Before the Gold Rush." *British Columbia Historical Quarterly*. Vol. 2, No. 4 (October 1938): 246-264.

McDonald, Neil and Alf Chaiton (Eds.). *Egerton Ryerson and His Times*. Toronto: Macmillan, 1978.

McLarty, S. D. *The Story of Strathcona School, 1873-1961*. Vancouver: Vancouver School Board 1961.

Norton, Wayne. "The Cache Creek Provincial Boarding School, 1874-1890." *British Columbia Historical News*. Vol. 29, No. 2 (Spring 1996): 30-33, 40.

Ontario Royal Commission on Learning. *Report of the Royal Commission on Learning: For the Love of Learning: A Short Version*. Toronto: Queen's Printer, 1994.

Ormsby, Margaret. *British Columbia: A History*. Vancouver: Macmillan, 1958.

Ovans, Charlie. "The School System and School Administration: Past, Present and Future." *Eight Annual Conference of the British Columbia Principals' and Vice-Principals' Association, 13-16 October 1976, Powell River, B.C.*

Peebles, Harry M. "Administrators in Command." *Seventh Annual Conference of the British Columbia Principals' and Vice-Principals' Association, 15-18 October 1975, Fairmont Hot Springs, B.C.*

Persky, Stan. *Son of Socred.* Vancouver: New Star Books, 1979.

Raptis, Helen. "Dealing with Diversity: Multicultural Education in British Columbia, 1872-1981." Unpublished Ph.D. dissertation, University of Victoria, 2001.

Roy, Patricia E. (Ed.). *A History of British Columbia: Selected Readings.* Toronto: Copp Clark Pitman, 1989.

Sandison, James (Ed.). *Schools of Old Vancouver.* Vancouver: Vancouver Historical Society, 1971.

Sandwell, R.W. (Ed.). *Beyond the City Limits: Rural History in British Columbia.* Vancouver: University of British Columbia Press, 1999.

Segger, Martin and Douglas Franklin. *Victoria: A Primer for Regional History in Architecture.* Watkins Glen, New York: American Life Foundation and Study Institute, 1979.

Sheehan, Nancy M., J. Donald Wilson, and David C. Jones (Eds.). *Schools in the West: Essays in Canadian Educational History.* Calgary: Detselig, 1986.

Smith, Peter Lawson. *Come Give a Cheer. One Hundred Years of Victoria High School, 1876-1976.* Victoria: Victoria High Centennial Committee, 1976.

Stephenson, Penelope. "'Mrs. Gibson looked as if she was ready for the end of term:' The Professional Trials and Tribulations of Rural Teachers in British Columbia's Okanagan Valley in the 1920s." In Jean Barman, Neil Sutherland, and J. Donald Wilson (Eds.). *Children, Teachers and Schools in the History of British Columbia.* Calgary: Detselig, 1995, 235-257.

Stevens, Julie. "Letters from Montney: An Insight into the Rural Teaching Experience in Early Twentieth-Century British Columbia." *British Columbia Historical News.* Vol. 34, No. 2 (2001): 17-25.

Stortz, Paul J. and J. Donald Wilson. "Education on the Frontier: Schools, Teachers and Community Influence in North-Central British Columbia." *Histoire sociale/Social History.* Vol. 26, No. 52 (November 1993): 265-290.

Sturhelm, Yvonne. "Just or Unjust? The 1895 Dismissal of School Principal Joseph Irwin." *Okanagan History* 62 (1998): 44-53.

Sutherland, Neil. *Children in English Canadian Society. Framing the Twentieth Century Consensus*. Toronto: University of Toronto Press, 1976.

-------- "The Triumph of Formalism: Elementary Schooling in Vancouver from the 1920s to the 1960s." *BC Studies*. Nos. 69-70 (Spring-Summer 1986): 175-210.

-------- "'Everyone Seemed Happy in Those Days': The Culture of Childhood in Vancouver Between the 1920s and the 1960s." *History of Education Review*. 15 (1986): 37-51.

-------- "'One, Two, Three Alary:' Vancouver School Grounds Between the 1920s and the 1960s." *British Columbia Historical News*. Vol. 22, No. 2 (Spring 1989): 37-51.

-------- "'I can't recall when I didn't help:' The Working Lives of Pioneering Children in Twentieth-Century British Columbia." *Histoire sociale/Social History*, Vol. 24 (November 1991): 263-288.

-------- *Growing Up: Childhood in English Canada from the Great War to the Age of Television*. Toronto: University of Toronto Press, 1997.

Toutant, Tara. "'Whoever has knowledge has the future at his feet:' The Canadian Educational Response to the Sputnik Crisis." Unpublished paper, University of Victoria, 1993.

Tyack, David B. *The One Best System: A History of American Urban Education*. Boston: Harvard University Press, 1974.

Tyllinen, Seija. "The History of the Separation of Principals from the British Columbia Teachers' Federation." Unpublished M.A. thesis, University of British Columbia, 1988.

Ungerleider, Charles S. "Globalization, Professionalism, and Educational Politics in British Columbia." *Canadian Journal of Educational Administration and Policy*. No. 9 (15 December), 1996.

Van Brummelen, Harro. "Shifting Perspectives: Early British Columbia Textbooks from 1872-1925." In Nancy M. Sheehan, J. Donald Wilson, and David C. Jones (Eds.). *Schools in the West: Essays in Canadian Educational History*. Calgary: Detselig, 1986, 17-38.

Waites, K.A. (Ed.). *The First Fifty Years: Vancouver High Schools, 1890-1940*. Vancouver: Vancouver School Board, 1941.

Waller, Willard W. *The Sociology of Teaching*. New York: Wiley, 1932.

Warburton, Rennie. "The Class Relations of Public School Teachers in British Columbia." *Canadian Review of Sociology and Anthropology*. Vol. 23, No. 2 (1986): 210-229.

Warren, Bob. *The George Jay School, 1909. A Glance Back at Elementary Public School Education*. Victoria: Published by author, 1998.

Wilson, J. Donald. "The Visions of Ordinary Participants: Teachers' Views of Rural Schooling in British Columbia in the 1920s." In Patricia Roy (Ed.). *A History of British Columbia: Selected Readings*. Toronto: Copp Clark Pitman, 1989, 239-244.

---------- "'I am Here to Help if You Need Me:' British Columbia's Rural Teachers' Welfare Officer, 1928-1934." *Journal of Canadian Studies*. Vol. 25, No. 2 (Summer 1990): 265-290.

---------- and David C. Jones (Eds.). *Schooling and Society in Twentieth-Century British Columbia*. Calgary: Detselig, 1980.

---------- and Paul J. Stortz. "'May the Lord Have Mercy on You:' The Rural School Problem in British Columbia in the 1920s." *BC Studies*. No. 79 (Winter 1988-89): 24-58.

Wotherspoon, Terry. "British Columbia Public School Teachers." *BC Studies*. 107 (Autumn 1995): 30-59.

Young, G.M. *Victorian England: Portrait of an Age*. London: Oxford University Press, 1960.

Yri, Marlene. "The British Columbia Teachers' Federation and Its Conversion to Partisanship, 1966-972." Unpublished M.A. thesis in Political Science, University of British Columbia, 1979.

Index